E N D

"For nearly 25 years, I have benefited from a relationship with Tom Atema – not simply because of our friendship and shared values, but also from his expertise in leadership skills, organizational development, and donor related ministry experience. Tom is not only an expert in best practices, he is a creative thinker and a healthy risk taker. Those are qualities I have long observed and admired.

In his new book, *"Relationships Break the Rules: Rethinking Our Non-profit Mandate",* we now have a primer on Tom's organizational development prowess. His secret has been a focus not on the gift in ministry, but the donor who offers that support. He has championed the "added value" of relating to and caring for the donor first – before an ask is even contemplated. And ... even before those relationships with investors in ministry are considered, Tom details the need for being certain that the team of co-workers are encouraged too! He reflects a Biblical understanding of ministry, teamwork, and the necessity of engaging donors – one personal relationship at a time!

In reading this book, I feel that Tom is relating directly to me. His style is personal, his words are targeted, and his own experiences are enlightening. Even through this book – Tom purposes to engage the reader personally – and in doing so has "added value" to me and any other reader that delves into this challenge. In the end – Tom purposes that ministry efforts including fund raising – all begin and end with relationships. That is the power of a Christian witness, a ministry focus, and a stewardship principle – and after all, that is just like Jesus!

Engage this book – it just may change the way you relate to each day, each ministry engagement, and each organizational plan. You will be glad you did!"

David Bruce
Executive Vice-President,
Billy Graham Evangelistic Association
Montreat, North Carolina

"This book will set you on a new path by showing you a new way to think! Tom Atema shows the reader how to focus on the relational, he calls it an art. Think about it—if we can maneuver from the mere transaction to the movement of an art, we have engaged something special. A mere transaction is at best boring but the relational investment into people, well that is both exciting and fun!

The value of people, love, celebration, teams—begins with knowing who you are. It boils down to addressing Tom's comment: "the difference between managing your relationships and playing the fundraising game requires a persistence self-check of your own motives"—in other words why are you doing what you are doing? No wonder Jesus deduced the entire Old Testament law into Love God and Love Others—if you are motivated from this space you are on the right path. Invest in others by reading Tom's book, you might just find the transformation you have been searching for. And I would bet you will enjoy the process of rethinking!"

Kathleen Patterson, Ph.D.
Professor, Director,
Doctorate of Strategic Leadership Program
School of Business & Leadership
Regent University

TOM ATEMA

with MIRIAM DRENNAN

RELATIONSHIPS
BREAK THE
RULES

RE-THINKING OUR
NON-PROFIT MANDATE

dustjacket

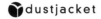

DEDICATION

This book is dedicated to all those relational
people in non-profits who know the benefit
of adding value to people.

CONTENTS

INTRODUCTION.. xi

ONE: WHAT ABOUT THE PROCESS?..................... 1

TWO: RE-THINKING WHAT WE VALUE 7

THREE: ALL, ALL IN 15

FOUR: WHAT GOT YOU HERE WON'T
GET YOU THERE 31

FIVE: IT'S ALL ABOUT A RELATIONSHIP 51

SIX: A WARNING TO NON-PROFITS,
FAITH-BASED AND SECULAR 71

SEVEN: EVERYONE KNOWS IT, SO WHY
ARE YOU TALKING ABOUT IT?..................95

EIGHT: OBJECTIONS, CORRECTIONS, AND
AUTHENTIC CONNECTIONS 117

A FINAL NOTE FROM TOM.. 147

ABOUT THE AUTHOR... 155

INTRODUCTION

Is fundraising an art, or is it a science?

This is a question I am asked quite often, and it always leads to an interesting conversation.

I will not deal with the term *fundraiser* here as I cover this throughout the book—except to say, why would you want to be a *fundraiser*? Anyway . . .

One reason I wrote this book is because as I speak with people every day and it is obvious to me that we have lost the art of building relationships. The art of building relationships, as you will read in this book, is not complicated; you just need to consistently add value to those in your path, and not think about how you'll benefit from it. Relationships—and being relational—cannot be a strategy to get something.

Way too many non-profits define their ministry success largely on how the financial reports look. What that means is that their success is based on how eloquently they ask, using their well-practiced technique(s), and how well they know the science, because science equals results. If they check all these boxes, then the funds will just roll in . . . because they followed the 'science' of fundraising.

If you follow the science, then you're transactional. No matter what word you place before the word *transactional*, you work in a world of science. If you do this, science tells you your outcome. Unfortunately, you'll also never stop running your scientific experiments.

If you're relational, however, your passion is the art. The more you pour yourself into a relationship, the more beautiful that piece of art becomes; relationships should add value to your investor, and just by that person being in your life, you and your organization will benefit, as well, because of The Law of Reciprocity. It's the art of adding value to people that's the key in relationships.

I believe that the "fundraising" industry experts and practitioners are on both sides of the fence; so, is fundraising an art or a science? You might think you have to decide which one is the best direction for your organization.

True, some try to do both. They combine the art *and* the science. If you study these, you will find a few interesting facts:

- More times than not, non-profits who say they are "balanced" between art and science tend to lean far more into science than the art.

- Non-profit organizations like the lip-service of relationships; however, that's really more a justification in their own minds than day-to-day practice. You've seen it all before. They share a fantastic story; chalk it up to "relational" (the art); mix in a heavy dose of compelling data analysis and "optimization" (the science); and wonder why the results are not what they expected. Telling a story is *not* relational!

More and more non-profit organizations adopt "data-driven" mindsets, in part because 21st century non-profits have more data than ever at their fingertips. Boards and other leaders desire "metrics" and "data" to validate where the budget is, where the non-profit is going, and what will be spent when and where. With metrics and data, they can justify their forecasts and be excellent in their own oversight. In its purest form, there is nothing wrong with forecasting; however, if this goes unchecked, or becomes out of balance, it becomes a slippery slope to deeper transactional activities. So, the real question they should be asking is, *How can we do more with less money?* Let's forecast that.

In each meeting and conversation, boards also need to ask themselves and their chief steward, *How are we adding value to people?* This is the art; the science is always self-explanatory. Art is *not* fundraising—period!

When non-profit organizations adopt "data-driven" mindsets, this thinking means that fundraising is just that . . . *fundraising.* Its dependence is far more on the science than the art. Yes, you need to know the science of the industry for sure. This data (science) needs to stay in-house and used very seldomly. It must never be used to drive our conversations, but it is, however, important to add another phrase to the conversation: "evidence-based," as a friend of mine calls it. What does *evidence-based* mean in the non-profit context? Evidence-based relates to what we want to *accomplish* through financial resources. What does the evidence of their investments show? The answers to these questions only come by holding many conversations.

Science has a place here. If we follow the science, what do investors see? Research (science) shows us that investors are drawn to non-profits whose representatives:

- have a passion for their organization
- exude a high level of energy
- listen well
- demonstrate deep integrity
- dislike the status quo and have a solution
- love their work
- go the extra mile for them time and time again

Do you see anything about money or finances in the list above? No. Investors care about the person and the relationship they have with them. As non-profit leaders, why would we prioritize any differently?

Yes, you need to know the science behind your work; however, that cannot drive you. No question, you can live in this science-space and follow the rules, receiving a check or two to make or exceed your budget. If you lack the art of a relationship, though, you will lose self-respect, and miss ninety-nine percent of the equation.

Our core belief, our relationships—adding value to others—is what we are called to do. This is our mandate; it's time we re-think it, and break a number of our non-profit "rules" along the way.

ONE

WHAT ABOUT THE PROCESS?

In 2018, I took notice of how much—and how well—organizations celebrate the end game (their "win," their mission). In each of the board meetings I attended that year, we spent time reviewing the financial budget, as we should have, to determine whether we met our goals and had any shortfalls. We spent additional time listening to reports on what was done and, in a few cases, heard some great impact stories that were sprinkled in. As I listened to these reports, I remember thinking all of this is great, necessary, and part of our responsibilities as a board . . . but what about the process? *Why are we not talking about, and evaluating, the process?*

I carried this thought with me into the next couple of years, in a number of board meetings at various non-profits. During that time, the thought hit a crescendo: WHY ARE WE NOT TALKING ABOUT THE PROCESS? Not long after that, I received my answer.

In late 2020, I visited a foundation and was making conversation with their leadership team while waiting for the meeting to start. Over time, I'd gotten to know most of them quite well, so the conversation was easy and informal. At one point, the head of the foundation looked at me and he said, "Tom, out of the hundreds of clients who send proposals or make presentations, you're the only one who does not ask for money. When we talk, it's clear that you care about me as a person. People have lost the art of building relationships."

A DETOUR INTO MY PAST

Now I'll admit this wasn't always the case. In fact, there was a time when I tried to be just the opposite—and admittedly, it was uncomfortable. Early on, I worked for a non-profit organization that fits the description of my friend's other clients. I thought asking for money was what I was supposed to do, and my success was largely in how eloquently I asked. If I had the technique, knew the game, the checks would just roll in . . . right?

That meant generating a lot of proposals and presentations, learning the jargon, and all of it focused on one thing: raising money. More than once I was instructed to, "Go visit the John Does and bring back a check." Yes, the directive was that blatant.

On one occasion, I arrived at the appointment time, rang the doorbell, and finally, the husband opened the door. Instantly, I knew he'd forgotten our appointment—this was way before cell phones and text messaging, so we didn't have the conveniences of text or email notifications. Peering inside his home, I could see his wife at the kitchen table. I knew by their puffy eyes and tear-stained faces that something was very wrong.

Without thinking about the check—my purpose for being there—I engaged in a totally different conversation than I had planned. Turns out my instincts were right. After listening to them pour out their hearts, I tried to encourage them and made sure I prayed with them before I left. I left without a check—in fact, I never mentioned the ministry or our needs in our conversation that day.

When I returned, my boss greeted me with, "How much is the check?" *Gulp.*

Now in all fairness, the pressure was on—our organization needed a lot of checks, and fast. But I realized that this 'transactional fundraising' that most non-profits do wasn't fulfilling, and it certainly wasn't sustainable. If we're here to help each other, truly be there for one another, how can we do that without a relationship? And without a relationship, how do we know whether we want to work with those individuals, or if they want to work with us?

I would like to say the lightbulb turned on in my head at that exact moment, but I was too busy listening to my boss's harsh words about my empty hands and check-less pockets. That particular incident did get my wheels turning a bit differently, however, about what I was doing, why I was doing it, and—the biggie—*how* I was doing it.

What about the process?

In my own experience, most fundraisers—development directors, managers of financial resources, tangible kindness executives, whatever fancy way we're referring to them now—dislike transactional fundraising. They know this model puts them on a road to nowhere—even if they meet their numbers. It's a temporary fix, no matter what.

It's a vicious cycle, set on repeat, each month, each quarter, each year.

Since fundraisers don't really enjoy rejection, transactional fundraising is actually easier for them, because it creates a barrier . . . and hey, it worked last month, so it must be the successful way to ask. Right? They struggle to imagine what it could be like to build sincere relationships with people they do not know at all. Way too many feel safer with the arm's-length, one-size-fits-all communications printed (or emailed) ask.

Then, as the transactions occur, they get addicted. They get hooked, thinking it's successful, and it becomes the only way non-profits and faith-based organizations know how to meet their budgets. Lather, rinse, repeat.

RELATIONAL FUNDRAISING DOESN'T EXIST

"People have lost the art of building relationships," my friend repeated. "You know where the line is, and you don't cross it."

"What do you mean?" I asked.

"You don't want to go to my kids' weddings. You don't ask to have dinner with me every time you're in town. But you truly care about me and what's going on in my life. I can tell if people play the game of relationships—they're either too far away or too deep and familiar. You care enough to know where the line is—and it's authentic. You should write a book about this."

Except that relational fundraising doesn't exist. In fact, it's an oxymoron. That's okay, I like a good challenge.

And clearly, since you're reading this, I accepted the challenge.

So if I'm writing about something that doesn't exist, it might be wise to clarify some terminology. *Relational fundraising* is an oxymoron, because if you're *fundraising*, you're raising funds. You're not thinking about the other person. You're not really being relational. If you're relational, you want something for the other person and you're not in it to raise money.

We have to re-think relationships and fundraising. So, what do I mean by *relational funding*? The short answer: You're either relational, or you're not.

Now, there is such a thing as *relational transaction* or a transactional relationship. These are 'in-the-moment' sorts of transactions that may affect your decision-making. My wife, for example, likes Aldi's. In a pinch, if we're starving, we'll buy food wherever we can, but given a choice, my wife will go to Aldi's because of the woman at the register. She's kind, she's happy, and always upbeat. It's a transactional relationship—but it's not relational fundraising.

If you don't want a relationship unless you get something in return—that's not relational, either. Even if you golf with your largest donors at your organization's golf scramble and take them to dinner afterward, that's not what I mean when I talk about being relational.

A relational person is intentional about their 'why' when they connect with people. I'm not talking about playing a game—more on that later—but a truly relational person will care more about that other person than they do for themselves. It's more *we* than *me*, and not about what you and I, as non-profit leaders, get out of the relationship. If you're a relational person, you are always asking yourself, *What can I do to add value to that other person?*

It's an honest investment. You see, we will never arrive at unity until we arrive at agreement. We'll never arrive at an agreement until we understand where people are coming from. And we are not going to understand where people are coming from until we sit down, stop criticizing them, and connect with them instead.

As leaders in the non-profit world, we have a responsibility to think and steward differently. This requires us to think deeply about people, and think ahead of people. I'm writing this to help you start thinking and stop copying what everyone else has been doing.

This book is not about how to hold onto the status quo, nor how to be "successful." You're not going to find the "keys" or "must-do's" for raising the funds you need to accomplish your organization's mission. If you're here to learn how to get better at the fundraising game, this is not the book for you. If you're weary of stressing about budgets and want to be released from that mindset, keep reading.

I am humbled to share with you some key thoughts that I believe will help all organizations, faith-based or non-faith-based, re-think the path they are taking in accomplishing their respective missions. I'll share some triumphs and challenges I've encountered in my own 30+ years of experience, along with some tools to help you—as my friend put it—care enough to know where the line is.

This is our mandate. Are you ready to re-think it?

TWO

RE-THINKING WHAT WE VALUE

M any years ago, I accepted a role to manage a radio station that, at the time, was-transactional in their funding efforts. I mean, we're talking *transactional* with bold red letters, underlined, in flashing neon lights.

I have already mentioned that once upon a time, I worked hard to be transactional, thinking that was who I needed to be in order to do my job as a fundraiser successfully. There wasn't some lightbulb moment where I switched to being relational. It was more of a progression that started way back when I first entered the faith-based career world, and I had to raise support for my family. Every time I went to churches and civic groups to present what I was doing to help young people, I felt like I was selling something, and it just irritated me . . . but I didn't know why.

So maybe it wasn't a lightbulb moment, but it certainly was a catalyst. I realized there is a difference between valuing people and adding value to them versus getting what you want, or even what you need. It was a progression, but I decided to be very intentional about adding value to people *first*, and caring about what they cared about *more* than what I cared about at any given moment. Being relational means that I am always authentically curious about the other person who comes across my path. *What breaks their heart? What do they sing about? What's bothering them? What's their dream?*

This seems counterintuitive, particularly for those of us who work in ministry or non-profits. We think that because we need money, we need donors, right? No, I intentionally shift my thinking to caring for others first. I have to care about what they care about. I want to understand them, in order to develop a relationship with them.

Just in case you missed it in the previous chapter: *We will never arrive at unity until we arrive at agreement. We'll never arrive at an agreement until we understand where people are coming from. And we are not going to understand where people are coming from until we sit down, really listen, stop criticizing, and connect with them instead.*

I'll add: *When we connect with them, we have the opportunity to add value to them.*

By the time I arrived at the radio station, I had a relational mindset and quickly surmised they were all about transactions. We took two years and a heck of a lot of patience—*we*, because it required the leadership team—to turn it around and build a relational environment that became part of our DNA.

Because we value people above all else, we started by coordinating a prayer team. From there, we imagined, dreamed, and incorporated a number of other small, personal touches to show listeners and the community that we cared. Not because we wanted or needed money—but we wanted to care for and about them. No one developed a flow chart or algebraic equation that said, "if we do X, Y number of times, we'll get Z." That's not at all what I mean by intentional or relational.

We weren't trying to shove something down their throats. We told our story, which included our mission and vision, and we mentioned what God was doing around the world. We asked the audience to tangibly get involved with some of the mission projects that we were involved in. Yes, we encouraged them to get involved—but not necessarily by writing a check. As a result, eight thousand unused wheelchairs went to those in need; twenty thousand CDs went to African radio stations; eyeglasses went to China; used Bibles went to China, notes and all; and of course, there were any number of local homeless shelters and rescue missions in our listening area that had needs we felt—with the help of our listeners—we could fill.

What happened next shouldn't have taken us by surprise, since we were faith-based—but nonetheless, God never ceases to amaze. All of a sudden, the funds started coming in for the station itself. The law of momentum kicked in, and we received two million dollars in two days during a special annual event.

Now when others tell this story, they speak about how we "raised two million in two days," but they forget one important piece: we'd spent the past four years building and cultivating authentic relationships with those whose passions aligned with ours.

THE MANDATE

Just like relational fundraising doesn't exist, adding value to people isn't an elaborate strategy to meet your financial goals (I can't stress this enough, so prepare to hear it a lot throughout this book). The Westminster Catechism states that Christ died for *people*—not your budget, décor, etc. His sacrifice added to our value, making us heirs to his kingdom. We didn't write him a check, nor did he ask us for one. All he has asked for is the opportunity to enter into a relationship with us—one that is not forced, scheming, or seasonal.

He did leave this earth with one mandate for those who *do* have a relationship with him: "A new commandment I give unto you, That ye love one another; as I have loved you, that ye also love one another," (John 13:34, KJV).

Look back at that verse from the Book of John. Now take the word *love* and replace it with the word *value* (I'm not attempting to change scripture here, but to further underscore my point). It says something like: *I added value to you, add value to others, just as I value you*. In his earlier teachings, Christ explained that taking care of our neighbors is the best way to value people. So a friend asked him, "Who is my neighbor?"

Christ responded with the parable known as "The Good Samaritan" to not only respond to his question, but to illustrate how this might play out in daily life.

We all have our moments when we are the first passers-by in the parable—we know better, should help when we see the need, and should steward our lives better in order to carry out this mandate of love and value. Instead, we are wrapped up in *self*—self-interests, self-service, and even self-righteousness. When the Samaritan arrives on the scene—someone who culturally would have been abhorrent to the Jews whom Jesus was teaching—we see how the Samaritan stewarded his life really well. Not necessarily because he took care of the guy on the side of the road, which was an extraordinary act of kindness; rather, because he went above and beyond the basics. Not only did he get him off the side of the road, he took him to a place that was safe so that he could heal comfortably, and took care of all of his needs—medical, physical, emotional. On top of that, he returned to follow up with the guy and pay for any additional expenses incurred. He had the money; he didn't have to go find it, raise it, or concoct an elaborate strategy to secure it. He had stewarded it, and his life, really well. He valued people over customs, cultures, and rules that have the propensity to harden one's heart.

As Jesus concluded this story—and just in case anyone missed the point—he explained that our 'neighbor' is anyone who comes across our path. The mandate is not about them, as far as their politics, their skin color, their background, their beliefs; the mandate is about *us*, our actions, our behaviors, our hearts, toward them. If we believe Jesus is who he says he is, and commit to be his representatives while we're here on earth, what will we do to care for, and care about, them?

Using Christ himself as our model, examine the instruction in James 2:1: "My brethren, have not the faith of our Lord Jesus Christ, *the Lord* of glory, with respect of persons," (KJV). With respect to the King's English, this verse packs a whollop with regard to how we're supposed to live, but it finishes by telling us to treat everyone equally and with respect. There's nothing in there about profits, budgets, marketing strategies, or capital campaigns.

Yes, I'm a person of faith. Everything I do is put through my faith lens—I try to do this in every area of my life. I can't unscramble my faith from my life, or compartmentalize it. Looking back at how Jesus modeled this, we are to value *people*, all people, not just those who think, believe, or look like us. Even if you're not a person of faith, why wouldn't you value people and want to add to their value?

I value people because Jesus values people. But what does that really mean?

FRIENDLY VS. RELATIONAL

Are you relational, or are you friendly? There is a difference.

Lots of people are friendly, but they're not relational. A friendly person is somebody you connect with really well. They meet you, and you have a great conversation. You may even walk away thinking, *Well, that was a great conversation*. That's not a relationship. That's not even building a relationship. That's being friendly.

A relationship is repeatedly conversing with them and helping them because you *want* to encourage them. You encourage them because you want to add value to them. You have no other interest beyond that—there's nothing in it for you, you don't have a hidden agenda. You simply nurture this person because they are a fellow human being and you enjoy spending time with them.

For example, there's a gentleman I meet each week for breakfast. We have some common passions, some common interests, and I'm adding value to him. That excites me. And it excites him. That's a whole different level beyond just being friendly.

If you're an extrovert, you might think that relationships come easily, but think again; in fact, relationships actually come easier with an introvert, because they're willing to sit and spend hours one-on-one, learning and seeking to understand the other person. The problem is none of us like to be called out for *not* being relational. That's a stigma that we put on our society. So let's not get too hung up on the label of *relational*, or even the word *relationship*—it's far more important that we value others and add value to them.

Think about it: If we get into an argument over words and labels, we've missed the point entirely about what it means to be relational. You're not adding value by getting into an in-depth argument that has no resolve. Sure, you can voice your opinion and articulate your thoughts, but be mindful to steward that conversation in care and in valuing them as a person. If you have stewarded that value, that relationship, they'll remember that conversation and give you a call when they want to pick up the relationship again.

THREE
ALL, ALL IN

Whe n word got out that the radio station had "raised two million in two days," it was difficult to contain the truth of that timeline. I started getting requests from other non-profits and ministries, wanting to know how we did it. Even our local PBS station called me.

There is no formula to suddenly "be relational"—you're either relational, or you're not. Nonetheless, one ministry called and asked me if I could help them move from transactional fundraising to relational funding (note the words I'm using here, because "relational fundraising" doesn't exist). I was more than happy to work with them to integrate a shift in perspective that would, ultimately, permeate their entire organization. We worked for several months, starting at the individual level of their leadership team, to give them council on how they relate to their internal and external teams.

Even small steps, like no longer using the word *donors* and replacing it with the word *investors*, provided small, gradual shifts in mindset. It was going well until . . . well, it didn't.

One of their team leaders said, "No way. We like what we're doing. We're not going to put the work in to be relational in our fundraising. . . . We're already relational." The rest of the organization knew they weren't, but this leader didn't see it for himself. Remember what I said about friendly versus relational? Just because you're talking doesn't make you relational. And as a result, their efforts didn't work.

It's still a fine organization, and they have great funding results, but they're not a relational organization. They continue to ask for money month after month, quarter after quarter, year after year.

A relational mindset will not work at the organizational level if all *of you are not* all in. Read that statement again.

Here are five benchmarks to help you get there:

1. If you're a person of faith, you need to really study this and be convinced with your whole heart and mind. This is your mandate, and your heavenly father is calling you to do this.

2. You need someone, maybe from the outside of the organization, to help you walk the journey and talk you off the ledge when you teeter out there during the difficult periods.

3. You need your board chair and the rest of the board members behind you, because it's not going to be easy to make a switch from transactional to relational. Everyone needs to expect to take at least eighteen months to two-and-a-half years.

4. You must be intentional.

5. A relational mindset must be infused into the whole organization. It has to become the cultural DNA of your organization.

One team member cannot fly the relational flag for the entire team. The work starts at the individual level with the chief steward, and within the leadership team. This requires a willingness to examine flaws and faults you'd rather not look at, and likely think you've hidden from others. I'm here to tell you that you are kidding yourself if you think they don't show up, one way or another. It also requires a great deal of humility, which may mean a few policy changes here and there, and keeping your ego in check, but I don't want to get ahead of myself.

A few questions to honestly ask yourself:

- How do I value myself?

- What do I value currently, and what *should* I value as a chief steward of the organization? (Hint: I hope both answers are the people around you.)

- Do I refer to them as staff, team, or associates? (It makes a big difference. It tells a whole lot about what you think about relationships.)

- Do I conduct yearly performance reviews, or on-the-spot reviews? (It tells a lot about how relational you are now.)

You don't have to be outgoing or an extrovert to be relational. You can be an introvert, but your organizational DNA, your organizational structure, how you behave has to *be* relational. You cannot just *do* relational. Relational fundraising will not work; it doesn't exist. It's like pulling a paragraph out of a whole book—it's not the whole story.

WAIT, WHAT ABOUT THE PROCESS?

A lot (if not most) non-profit and ministry organizations would say they value people. Since non-profits are about making at least one aspect of people's lives better, they would say something like, "Of course we value people. We help them get out of poverty/help them learn additional skills so they can find work/be self-sustaining, and help them find eternal hope."

Let's word this a little differently, then: What kind of *worth* do you place on people? Seems like a provocative statement, but be honest. Are there some people "worth" more to you than others?

As we walk in the process of our organizational win, the one word that keeps us focused is *intention*—our intention is to fulfill our mission. We need to be intentional about each step, without skipping any, that lead us to *who we are in the process* of getting to our win.

You see, it's not enough to simply report on the organization's mission wins; you must evaluate key steps in the journey. Spend time thinking, praying, and working on making each key step better. The foundational base that supports all the other steps is how you are adding value to others. Each step in the process must add value to people.

As you continue working on those areas where you personally can be more relational, this is where your board of directors can, as a governing board, add tremendous value. First and foremost, everyone needs to do some forward-looking evaluation by asking and questioning: *How are we valuing people and our associates as we move towards the mission win?*

Some of the answers may be difficult to hear, but hopefully they will provide opportunities to address. If you are not questioning the underpinning of your non-profit, you are taking the process for granted. You are likely skipping over the steps and not using the correct tone and verbiage necessary to reflect the actions of an organizational culture that values people.

My definition of leadership is stewardship. We have to steward our influence, responsibilities, and how we value someone as an associate. We have to value those who come across our path. This is why governing boards need to spend more time evaluating the path—the process— than they do the financial sheets. Spend some time asking: *How did we get to these positive financial numbers?* Too often, however, if those numbers indicate a positive upward swing, we just applaud, yell, scream, praise the Lord, and move on.

And to that, I say *no*.

You must go back and look at the past. If you've got dead or injured bodies all over the path that got you to that number, you've got a massive problem. If you haven't added value to people unconditionally, you've got a problem. If all the numbers are positive because we are people of value who add value to people, then it must be about *all* the people that God puts in our path. If we don't, we are off-course and need to re-think our path, our mandate.

Even if the numbers have turned downward you still must evaluate the path. Are you adding value to people—really? Remember what Peter Drucker said? "Leaders deal in reality."

A RELATIONSHIP STEWARD

We've all been in situations where someone is being nice to us because maybe we've been benevolent in the past, or we have the potential to be benevolent. Transactional thinkers usually consider that person to be more valuable, because they've given more. So how do you balance that? How do you govern that? Do you prioritize? Is there a hierarchy? How do you shift from thinking in terms of calculations and results versus building a relationship?

In the early days of intentionally becoming relational, this will seem like you're walking a tightrope or trying to stand up and walk in shoes that are way too big. One thing to be mindful of until it becomes a reflex: *A relationship steward does not calculate results.* Why?

The latest research says it takes 63 times to make something happen. In order to switch your current habits to relational habits, you're going to have to practice adding value to people and building relationships at least 63 times before it becomes a habit in your life. When it comes to stewarding a relationship, you must be intentional.

Even if you might have walked out of a budget meeting and the budget is way out of whack. Maybe you have overspent, there's no money in the kitty to cover it, and you're up against a hard wall. The last thing you want to do is make that call to your board chair. You're in deep weeds. All of a sudden unexpectedly, you take a phone call from someone of wealth. Our current habit would be, *I need help and they can bail me out.*

The temptation will always be there, but that's not being relational. At the beginning of a relationship, make it a practice to call them by their first name and say, "What can I help you with?" Be intentional about not mentioning your need, but in adding value to people.

Now, if this person brings up your need, mention it by all means, but don't shift gears and let it drive the conversation. We want to have the conversation that says, *How can I add value to you?* Think about how you can add value to whatever they're calling about—not just by answering their questions, but going beyond that and making them feel like they're worth four million bucks. *That's* stewarding a relationship—when you want something *for* them. Not *from* them.

Thinking always drives actions, every time. As a leader, if you're always wanting something else—always asking someone for something, like a check—your value and leadership will be spent that way, because that's what consumes your thoughts. Sadly, what you're doing is really more of a reaction to circumstances instead of a proactive, mindful lifestyle that adds value to others.

I want to be very careful about what I'm about to say next, but here goes: In a *collective* sense, we need to consider the image our respective organizations project. That image emerges from the individuals within it, and that image-bearing begins with you, the leader, the chief steward. If you're intentional about being relational, however, this is not just an image change—this must be a change in your heart and thought patterns.

From here, your word choices are not just important; they are *vital* to building and maintaining a relational culture, and reflect whether you truly value people. When you think of the word *staff*, for example, what comes to your mind?

- It indicates that each person around you is employed by the organization to do a specific job.

- It projects the image that your staff supports you, they are below you.

- It suggests they carry out the menial tasks so *you* can have an organizational win.

Staff are here to serve the leader so the leader can accomplish the mission. When you use the word *staff*, it reflects an operational mindset that suggests these individuals are easily disposable and exchanged, like a carton of milk or a box of tissues. These comparisons may seem extreme to you, but the word *staff* undermines the value of the person. It suggests that the leader and the organization really does not value them at the highest level possible; and trust me, the employees themselves are aware of it.

So, when we talk about a person's worth in relational terms, let's start with the people we work with. I call these individuals my "associates"—how do you refer to them, collectively? How much are they "worth" to you? Their worth is demonstrated by how you treat them and what you expect from them. The word *team*, or my preferred word *associate*, projects a totally different response and mindset. It really places each associate on the same esteemed level, equal to the chief steward. It is a conscious reminder that we value each person equally, regardless of responsibilities, education, or background. It sends the message that the organization cannot function properly without them, and they are highly valued.

I define an *associate* as two or more people who work *together* to achieve a common goal. Teams or associates offer an alternative to a vertical chain-of-command, and they offer a much more inclusive approach to the organization's win.

In fact, to take this one step further: Make your organizational chart circular, totally different than the "tree" look most use today. If that bruises your ego a bit, then you're on the right track. When your associates are regarded as equally important, then you are intentionally mindful of how you can add value to them, because they are key to the organization's win. The goal and the focus shift when you come to terms with it no longer being about you or that everything depends on you.

- Associates work and move in the same direction, together.

- Associates recognize they are not alone in this journey and respectfully steward each other's gifts, talents, and passions, while using their own with excellence.

- Associates recognize they are equally accountable to the organization's win, actively contribute to it, and therefore, the success is far more rewarding.

This mindset is central to your organizational culture, because your culture drives the vision. It determines whether you operate with passion, focus, and fun; it determines whether the win is considered a collective effort or the leader's glory.

HOW DO WE OPERATE WITHOUT BEING OPERATIONAL?

In a positive, open culture, communication with each associate is key. This is different than keeping score and tallying up all the positives and negatives for an annual performance review. Unless you must abide by them as a matter of policy, try to get away from doing them at all. If you're relational, you handle positive and negative conversations immediately and in-the-moment.

For example, every associate has blind spots (even you and me—sorry). When we have open, real-time conversations about these blind spots, we end up with a value-based culture.

How does this work? When we, or any associate, notices what someone else is unaware of (our blind spots) we speak up in the moment. When we speak up, we are intentional about being respectful, honest, and appropriately addressing the blind spot and only the blind spot. There is no "and another thing" to add to it. There are three reasons for this:

- It will help the person become more aware of what they do not know.

- It will help them move closer to fulfilling their dreams and the organization's dream.

- It will help you identify anything else you can do to help them, like additional training.

When I started being intentional about real-time conversations, everything changed—starting with the atmosphere—that led to a far better culture in the organization. With the situation fresh in our minds, we could both evaluate whether this was a win in light of what the associate was to accomplish, or a negative act that would affect the other associates and/or the mission win.

As soon as I noticed (or an associate noticed) a positive or a negative action, we would have a conversation. Together we came to one of two conclusions: We either celebrated the process towards the win so it became something really special for the associate (and an example for others), or we made the adjustments necessary so the person could become better. In both cases, it was a win not just for the associate, but for the culture and "win" of the organization.

In this culture of open communication, it also means anyone can come to me and have a conversation on anything they see that seems wrong or good. This not only benefits me to be better, it helps us "clear the air" and move forward as an organization.

Now, this next part is very important. Remember that circular organizational chart? When getting feedback of any type in a conversation, positive or negative, accept it from a neutral place and say, "Thank you." If you don't reply with a judgmental comment, you can't get into an argument that has no real winner or loser.

More than once after a meeting, an associate has come to me and asked, "Do you know what you said?" My response is usually *no*. They then pointed out to me that my actions indicated I had already decided before hearing everyone out, and that I was not really listening.

Another time, and this one's my favorite: When I have an answer and I'm ready to speak, my bottom lip quivers. I had no idea this was happening until it was pointed out to me. Now, many times when I am in a group meeting, an associate will just look at me and point to their lips, and I know what they are saying and I work on stopping those moving non-talking lips.

When we are relational, we value open and honest conversations—it's a value of our relational culture.

Real-time conversations make it easier for the associate to make corrective adjustments, personal or professional. It's easier to get better one small step at time than ask them to make a leap. This could sound like you're pushing the person all the time; if we really value our associates, however, we keep working with them to help them improve. If they're more efficient, they get the time back.

Frankly, I like to work toward giving my associates extra time. Extra time gives them the opportunity to work on a project that they are passionate about, maybe something that's not part of their organizational responsibilities. It could be part of something they dream about doing, are passionate about, but never "had the time."

For example, we may have associates who want to go on a church mission trip; we have it as part of our culture that they can go and it's not part of their vacation time. I can honestly say that each person who has done a special project has come back more passionate than before. In some cases, it has led to promotion or a redistribution of their responsibilities. The project made them better—far better. It's about adding value to them—first. The positive results will come and fall into place.

So even if your organization requires annual performance reviews, it is still better to have in-the-moment conversations with your team members. Why?

- Because every opportunity should be taken to develop your associates.

- Because you value the associate and the conversation proves it.

- Your associates are more apt to adjust faster and with far less resistance.

I have found when the system required a yearly review that I felt like a judge. The employee felt like they were on trial and it was never a great thing for either of us. "I have these four infractions to review with you—let's talk," never ends well for anyone. When we wait for the yearly review, we tend to let things slip or grow, and we are not helping the people around us get better. If your culture is one that values people, then have corrective conversations in the moment.

Now you may be thinking some of this seems airy-fairy and intangible, and it could be. However, it is actually very easy to measure the effects of a relational culture on your organizational win. Culture can be, and must be, measured.

When you have a culture that values people, it attracts potential additional associate members—and top talent comes your way. A sign your culture is weak or missing the mark is when no one is asking to join your team, or the selection pool is poor. Take a step back and review your applicants—if skills aren't matching or no one is knocking on your door, you know you have a culture problem.

By the way, this is also true when it comes to financial resources. Are people coming to you and saying something like, "I've heard about you or your organization and I want to see how I can help?" If that is not happening, you need to check your culture. More on this in Chapter 6.

I have the same belief about those yearly financial bonuses. If you notice, or the associates have noticed, a win, celebrate it along the journey to the win. It's far more meaningful. The fact is, when you do yearly bonuses, they are expected and not special; when families budget for them, it's proof they are not all that special as it relates to a job well done. If someone does an outstanding job, celebrate it in real time with the team. It makes a much larger impact in real time than to wait until Christmastime.

This is why we need to know their financial dreams as well, so we can help them move closer to reaching this dream or goal. The fact is, financial goals are, more often than not, tied to a personal dream.

With the mindset of an associate, you avoid the comparison trap. Instead, you celebrate each person's unique personality, talents, and skills that add jointly to the organization's win without comparing one associate to another. This, for me, is a highlight, and one of the true joys of leading.

ONE FINAL THOUGHT

As leaders, it is our privilege to steward each associate properly, whether their association is internal or external. Each one has been created for a purpose and the foundation of that purpose is to add value. We need to know their personal dreams, professional dreams, and financial dreams so we can see if there is a fit for them to fulfill their goals. We need to know our associates' personal dreams so we can enrich them in our organizational mission environment *and* they can accomplish all they were created to be.

Relationships are hard. We all know that they're extremely hard, but they are beneficial. The longer you invest in them, the more beneficial they become. The only way to grow an organization is by adding value to people. If the people around you are not growing, the organization is not going to grow, no matter what the financial numbers say.

FOUR

WHAT GOT YOU HERE WON'T GET YOU THERE

W hat got you here today won't get you there tomorrow, because we're not sure where 'there' is. One thing's certain, however: If we keep do- ing what we're doing today, even if we make today better, it's not going to allow us to accomplish what 'there' is.

You can break out all the data, charts, and graphs you want—none of them is a roadmap to 'there,' especially after a pandemic. All the data, charts, etc. can tell you is whether you're moving backward or forward financially. If you're wanting to shift to adding value with relation- ships, that requires you to re-think your process—or actually think about it in the first place—and do some things differently.

As leaders, we don't spend enough time, as chief stew- ardship officers of an organization, working *in* the process and in real strategic thinking *about* the process.

Recently, someone asked me, "What's the number one thing chief stewardship officers are doing now that COVID 19 is coming to an end?" And I thought to myself, *That's the wrong question*, especially in the context of how they asked. They knew I traveled a lot, working with various organizations, so it's true that I see a lot of initiatives. They were basically asking me, "I want to know what the hot thing is, so I can copy it and do it, too." That's not strategic thinking—that's copying. Even if you adjust it, tweak it, make it a little bit more your own . . . it's still somebody else's idea that was developed to fit their mission.

THE ADDICTION OF THE TRANSACTIONAL QUICK-FIX

When I was growing up, my father had a door-to-door milk route. He delivered the milk in glass bottles. As the industry moved away from glass bottles to cardboard containers, Dad invested in a few "milk-vending machines." Most of them were placed off to the side of an entrance to a gas station. You inserted your dime, and a quart of milk would drop out. It usually worked, and the machines required little-to-no maintenance beyond re-stocking.

Fundraising, for many, is a lot like those coin-operated vending machines. Send an email out and wow, money comes in—almost like magic. Transactional fundraising is easier, quicker, and it might feel good when you hit that threshold you're hoping for. But like any addiction, it's a quick fix and bad for you in the long-run; soon enough, you feel like you'll need those transaction hits every single day, and the machine kicks in.

When you live in this transactional world, you spend little or no time learning what the potential investor's personal goals are. What do they want to accomplish, professionally? What sort of family goals do they have? What are they most passionate about? Instead, many build a one-way transaction that often leads to a "you-owe-me" mindset. This is the idea that since 'they have money, they can help me,' and have little to no regard for them as a human being. Operationally, you will have the temptation to create a crisis each month to keep up with your addiction; you will always need more, because what comes in is never enough.

In the end, your organization's addiction to transactions ends up becoming unpleasant for the people who care about your mission the most. After all, those who invested with you were actually seeking to build meaningful relationships with your cause.

In fact, this might be the biggest reason organizations *stay* in the transaction mode. The leadership doesn't see relational results fast enough, so they become impatient. They demand another transactional marketing effort. They'll strategize to get the email out today, "let's use a 'match' this time, does anyone know of a crisis we can be part of?"

What's sad is that in most cases, this actually works.

While transactions might be a worthwhile framework at the *very beginning* of a relationship with an investor, it's a terrible structure to continue, and ultimately, it will not help you. The transactional fundraising model focuses on one thing: Bringing in the funds you need to do the organization's mission. Fundraising becomes more of a machine, more research-driven than adding value to others. It's not relational. It's not distinct. It's easy, quick, and no one has to interact with anyone. It's what everyone else is doing, sometimes just copied with your logo slapped on it.

You will never be at ease, or comfortably paced, with your associate and investor relationships, because there's always a new race to run. The chase will never, ever end.

It's a trap.

The latest research compiled with non-profit leaders suggest that the typical "fundraiser" has an average tenure of eighteen months or less. One study referred to fundraising staff positions as a "revolving door."This is a major problem on multiple levels. I wonder if the majority of the reason for the high turnover is because the focus is on raising funds and not on adding value to people and building relationships?

Instead, try re-thinking your relationships and how you are adding value to those relationships. And please, stop raising money!

THE BEAUTIFUL MESS OF
BEING RELATIONAL

Think about it: Anyone and everyone who comes across your path has relationship potential. I'm not saying they will all develop into relationships, but the *potential* is there. Wouldn't you rather find out for sure and not miss out on something exciting?

When you flex your relational muscles and work on developing this mindset, it still has to become part of your DNA. You have to own it. It's not a checklist, or how-to book; being intentional about being relational requires you to make it a part of your personal values. It's not a formula to be replicated or modified.

Unfortunately, for many of us in the non-profit world, when people come across our paths, what do we normally visualize, as though it's stamped on their foreheads? Dollar signs. We need to move to a point where we simply see a potential friend. Maybe not our best friend, but a friend just the same. Be okay with not knowing *why* they're in your path just yet, and trust that the reason is purposeful.

I'll put it to you a different way: Would you be more persuaded by someone who came to you and asked for something as a complete stranger, or would you be more persuaded to help after you get to know them?

VALUE EVERYONE
THE SAME WAY

It doesn't happen overnight. As soon as someone comes across our path, we have no way of knowing what will develop. But if we begin by seeing a dollar sign and placing value on them that way, you'll make an external judgment without knowing anything about them—besides their suit, their car, or maybe the kind of coffee they ordered. If you put a dollar sign on them, you're probably making a judgment that's way off-base anyway.

When you're a relational person, you're not after anyone's money, and you're not raising money. You accept that they crossed your path for a reason, and you want to find out more about them as a person. In the beginning, you stay in the neutral zone; when you move forward, there are no shortcuts. Relationships, genuine relationships, take time.

Usually, after a couple conversations, I know whether this is someone I'd like to engage with long-term; not to get them to do something for me, but because I desire something for them. I want to help them succeed, be fulfilled, and to accomplish all they were created to accomplish in life. I just want to connect and engage. Maybe they think differently, and they helped me think in a new realm. Maybe I find them encouraging or they said something that strengthened me in a particular area. I just like being around them, and wonder how I can add value to them. When we value people, it not only affects the way we treat the associates around us, it also affects the way we interact with those whom we come in contact. Our associates are a group of people who help our organization accomplish its organizational mission, regardless of *how* they do this. We should never limit this group to just those who are paid, or who volunteer for the organization. Include everyone that expresses interest of any kind.

It's no secret that every non-profit needs money. Unfortunately, we tend to skip over the 'add value to people and not worry about us' part and instead ask, "How many people can I send this email to so that we'll get the funding we need to accomplish the organization's mission or project?" More often than not, we "farm" a bought or borrowed email list, or use a collaborated list that seems like it's a semi-close fit for the organization.

The truth is, every non-profit organization *does* fundraise (more on this in Chapter 7), and each organization needs people to accomplish the resourcing goals. I know that people are the key here, we need to pause and spend time evaluating *how* you value the people who will fund your mission.

Call me a broken record, but I'll ask it again: *What about the process?*

If you're looking at it from a transactional standpoint, it's kind of like, *The first thing we do is we move them into the organization, and see what can they do for us?* And that's the wrong attitude to have, the wrong DNA for any organization to have.

Shouldn't we try to find out how they're wired, and what they believe, what their passions are? I find that out by asking questions; people love to answer questions. They love to talk about themselves and about what they think and believe. And if you ask people about themselves, *and listen intently*, they become your friend pretty darn fast.

Returning to the underlying philosophy of adding value to all people also includes those who help you have a missional "win." Think about what happens if you do not pay attention to this area.

There is a two-step process to add value to people in the area of gaining resources. Let me say upfront: It takes work, and it is very hard work. It takes a long-focused view that you will need to work on all day, every day—and I do mean, all day, every day.

IS IT A SCHEME,
OR DO YOU MEAN IT?

What I'm about to divulge is, unfortunately, not the normal mode of operation for non-profits. Most organizations' MO is all about getting money, including those in the faith-based world. Many non-profit organizations look from the outside-in, as a weak "get-rich-fast" scheme.

Now that I've gotten your attention: *Many of those who raise funds for their non-profit need to re-think their mandate.*

I do not believe any non-profit organization believes they operate, or want to be known as, a get-rich-fast organization; after all, their mission is just and noble. When it comes to funding that just and noble mission, however, there is a much different story to be told.

Non-profits need to operate in a counter-intuitive way to that norm. We need a mindset that communicates:

- We will not ask for money.

- We really do not want anything from the people who might (or do) fund us.

- We really mean both of those statements from the depths of our souls.

I know that for many of you, just reading those bullet points is painful. Others may have already closed this book. Some will say, *What's the catch?*

There is no catch. It's foundational for adding value to people. Do you really want something *from* someone? Or do you want something *for* the people that come into our path, first and foremost?

I want something for the person God has placed in my path—period. Nothing more.

A FEW TIPS FOR THE
SMALL-TALK CHALLENGED

Let's start with those random encounters we all have each day. Say I'm in a coffee shop and somebody behind me starts talking to me, I might ask them what they think of the weather—you know, "it sure is a nice day," or "think we'll float away in all this rain?" From there, I might engage further by asking them how their day is going.

Maybe I'm meeting someone for lunch. We might have set up this time on the phone, but we've never met in person. I might greet them, thank them for their time, and ask them what else is on their schedule that day. Eventually, we might talk about what we could "do over" from the previous day if we had the chance, or what we're most proud of, music tastes, etc. We might talk about what they do for fun, or maybe what they do to stay healthy, favorite authors, special travel destinations, you know, you go back and forth with every question going a little deeper. Pretty soon, you'll learn about their pet peeves or long-term goals. Maybe they're in a role that puts them in line for a larger, corporate job in a larger city. I might ask them about their plan and strategy to land that bigger role, and discuss why it's important to them.

There is no script—if there was a script, then you've missed the point. The conversation happens organically and you have to take each situation as it comes. You can gauge how to proceed based on how they respond; you'll know when they feel safe enough to go a bit deeper.

Here are a few more springboard questions to help you think of different questions to ask:

- Who are your favorite artists?

- Any of them a hero of yours? Why?

- If not, who is your hero?

- I see you live here in _____, have you always lived here, or are you a transplant?

- Have you lived anywhere else?

- Did you enjoy living there as a child?

- What made you move here?

- Where did you go to college?

RELATIONAL ACCOUNTABILITY

You may be wondering which is more important at this stage—our internal team, or external relationships?

God knows what we need and when we need it. He's responsible for supplying our needs, according to His will and His timing—and that even includes *not* funding us. My privilege, my responsibility, is to be accountable and value people first—which sets the table so God can do His best work. Internal teams, external relationships—we are to value them all. If you're intentional about being relational, you can't really compartmentalize the two, but our focus for this chapter is primarily on external relationships (we will address internal relationships in Chapter 5).

When someone crosses our path, we are accountable to steward the relationship to the best of our ability. To help enrich that person to be all they are created to be, and leave the rest to God. This is a mindset that needs to be evaluated daily. It takes a while to make this part of your DNA, both at the individual and organizational levels, as part of your values system.

By now, if you're thinking, "I like this strategy. We'll make an announcement and plan a rollout," then you're not there yet. You do not announce it. That is transactional.

The decision to be relational is intentional, yes—but it's personal. As you interact with your associates and investors, you'll find yourself using different words. In fact, that word—*associates*—may be one of the first changes you make. When people ask why you're suddenly using that word, you have the opportunity to tell them, "I really want to add value to you. I think *associate* better defines who we are, what our DNA should be, and what our culture should be."

This brings up the question of policy changes. You can't make it a policy or statement to be relational and expect it to be authentic. As you move toward a more relational approach, however, you may see some policies need adjusting to reflect who you are and add value to your associates. What's done internally will move almost seamlessly to the external.

As chief steward officer—and if you're the president, CEO, head honcho, I'm talking directly to you—the accountability starts with you. If you don't have integrity with yourself, you'll never have integrity with anyone else. You're accountable for setting the table so people can notice your organization's mission. You are accountable for this portion—God's responsible for sending the people. It will take multiple opportunities across multiple platforms for someone to take notice of, and be drawn to your organization.

Follow me here: Not every contact is an opportunity. Remember, you're accountable to attract the kind of person you desire to engage with. Tell stories that represent your organizational mission so that you will find people who align with your mission, and vice-versa.

Eighty percent of what your organization does is the same as other organizations, and they're doing it just as well, if not better, then yours. The difference will be found in the twenty percent—what makes your organization special. It's how you stand out—your distinction from the others. You and I need to work more in the twenty percent than in the eighty percent. Your associates do the eighty percent, and they need to be empowered to do their work with excellence and be accountable for it. Trust me, this is going to be more difficult than you think— it's way too easy, and disastrous, for you to drift into the eighty percent.

Instead, we need to focus on things like how we tell our stories in order to paint the proper picture of our respective missions, and do it better than anyone else. You'll remain on the cutting-edge because you have taken the time to think, re-think, take some risk, and to act differently . . . all within that twenty percent that makes you distinct from everyone else. Keep your thinking current, not in the past.

As soon as someone tells you, "everyone is doing this," it should be the first warning sign that it's time to re-think whatever it is and look at it differently. If everyone else is doing it this way, why do you want to do it this way? You're accountable to the twenty percent. People will find you because of the excellence of your twenty percent, not the eighty percent, regardless of how excellent the latter is. They are impressed with your story, your associates, your outcome, or something else that makes them take that second look. What they see grabs their attention.

After some thinking, they see a possible connection with their passion and it lines up with your mission. This is what I call a "passion-match," and it's an extraordinary relationship when it happens. Maybe they found you through a search of their passion on social media, or through their church, or a friend. Maybe they heard you on the radio, or on a TV interview you did about your mission. Maybe they saw your cause on YouTube. Any and all of these channels are vital to finding those who have a passion-match, and provide great opportunities for your organization to stand out and get noticed; they are essential to your twenty percent.

Now for some, this is where it ends. They think fondly of your organization and will speak highly of it to others. But for others, they connect and take the next step—to see if you are, in fact, what you claim to be. They want to get to know you better, and they will take action for you to notice them. They'll make their move by investing or volunteering, and hope the connection is strengthened. It's very similar to dating, actually; and how you respond determines whether you get that all-important second and third date.

In my fundraising philosophy, the "first date" is still transactional—it's one and done, and that's where the transaction ends. We walk this path to the "first date" as stewards who are accountable for our ministry. *How* we impress another person is key.

I won't ask the question this time, I will just state it: *It is about the process.*

We must spend a lot of time on these impressions, because we are accountable. The look, the wording, the calls, the thank-yous, the prayers . . . each one is a key portion of the twenty percent. Take the time needed to evaluate each step in the process, over and over again. Why?

If you do not pay attention to how you're adding value on a daily basis, you will slip back into fundraising mode very quickly and without even noticing it. Daily accountability helps you move to what I call the "engage stage," where you build and deepen the relationship. This is why I use the word *investor*, for example—it's a value-added word.

The terms *donate*, *fundraising*, and *development* relay the mindset that you give, I receive and spend, and that's it. It leads to a place where there is less accountability and transparency. It also can lead to a place where we become weak on producing the proper outcomes.

If I ask someone to *invest*, however, then their mind goes to Wall Street and financial portfolios. They may even ask me, "Will I get a return?" I respond with *yes*, which automatically positions us to be accountable and transparent, and encourages us to work accordingly to produce that proper return.

Make no mistake: In today's world, it is all about the story you are writing. People today desire to invest in your cause because it is a cause they feel passionate about, and they see that your organization is making great progress in this area. If your organization is in someone's ministry financial portfolio, it raises the stakes on your accountability and transparency.

A WORD SPECIFICALLY FOR FAITH-BASED ORGANIZATIONS

Faith-based organizations have a simple, yet more challenging level of accountability, because they are required to listen to God, and only God. It's very hard to be accountable and rely on God one-hundred percent of the time.

Yes, there will always be this internal tension between the need for resources and the accountability of adding value to people. Thankfully, we have several biblical examples that remind us that God must be at the center of each step in the process, and He will show up in incredible ways to meet our needs—He promised!

Most of us are familiar with Moses, who is found in the Old Testament, even if your only frame of reference is Charlton Heston's portrayal of him. Moses was the first one to raise money from people, encouraging them to give freely. God told Moses to "bring me an offering: of every man that giveth it willingly with his heart ye shall take my offering" (Exodus 25:1). Moses' solicitation was exactly what God told him to ask for, word-for-word (Exodus 35: 4-9; 25;3-7). He faithfully detailed the needed funds and then he listed the way those funds would be used. He even listed a requirement, that only those who "giveth it willingly with his heart" were to donate.

This appeal came right after the debacle of the golden calf, so they could have easily been led to give out of guilt. But take notice of one more item in Moses' appeal; they had been slaves in Egypt. They were skilled people, but they were still slaves; they did not have much money, and they were in the desert. I find it fascinating that Moses asked for a variety of gifts. It was not one-size-fits-all and gave more people the opportunity to be part of the blessing of meeting the goal. And the people responded in an incredible way; not only was the goal met, it was exceeded. Exodus chapters 25, 35, and 36 provide a very detailed account of how the gifts were used.

The offering was made to the Lord, *not* to the people of the tabernacle. In fact, this whole financial effort was God-centered; God was, and is, present in every step of the process. This account should reassure us of our steps today.

The New Testament gives us even more examples. When Jesus' followers in Antioch heard that a famine had hit the entire Roman Empire, without hesitation they collected funds to help the people most in need. Never before in history had a group felt responsible for an assembly far away from home. This was ground-breaking, because it was not politically, socially, or economically motivated; they did it because they understood God's love for the world and the new life they had because of that love. Now that love resided in them, and this is the sort of action love requires. This was a brand-new thing called *generosity*—something that would take care of physical and financial needs.

The Apostle Paul also had a lot to say about giving and asking for the gift—he wrote epistles. Letter-writing is still effective today; it is transactional, and usually called a "donor appeal letter." In fact, 1 Corinthians shows a reasonable, logical, proportional approach to systematic giving, which today we call automatic monthly giving, by credit card or EFT.

In 2 Corinthians, Paul even deals with the lapsed donor (see 8:11; 9:3). It's interesting that Paul initiates competitive giving with the Macedonian churches and those in Corinth. But then Paul adds something that was on his heart: "Not that I speak in respect of want: for I have learned, in whatsoever state I am, therewith to be content," (Philippians 4:11). Paul is telling us that *any* ministry that regularly employs a crisis tactic to raise funds should re-examine their heart. He is imploring those of us who steward these funds to watch our hearts, because we're accountable with what we do with them, but not responsible for them.

James speaks into treating everyone equally and not showing favoritism, a directive Paul also gives Timothy. Both apostles say we are not to look at people based on what they can do for us.

In fact, Paul reminds us that giving in any form should be done according to how and when hearts are moved to do so—not because they've been shamed, manipulated, or coerced: "Every man according as he purposeth in his heart, so let him give; not grudgingly, or of necessity: for God loveth a cheerful giver," (2 Corinthians 9:7, KJV). Giving is a heart-thing, not a duty to be performed.

When you look behind the curtain, not only did these men of faith have a deep personal relationship with God, each one lived in response to that relationship. They cared for their personal relationship with God *first*, and from that relationship they had a desire to want the best for the people around them. They stayed close to God, remained accountable to God, and God showed and told them what to do.

Their fundraising was God-directed; it got people's attention (they're accountable) and they responded (God's responsible). But do not miss this part: Moses, James, Paul, and others cared for the *relationship and the people more than the gift*. They were engaged with people, and wanted to see each person blessed and be all they were created to be. That could not happen until each party became engaged.

ENGAGEMENT ISN'T ONE AND DONE

In the non-profit world, two parties can notice each other and want to learn more from each other . . . but unless one of them (and in time, both of them) engages in a conversation and takes the initiative to make a move towards a "second date," you will never move forward in that relationship. Once they've given that first transactional "gift," they are now engaged with the organization. Are you interested in learning more about them, too? Likely, yes—so you respond and commit to move forward in an accountable way to learn more about the other person's dreams and passions.

Unfortunately, most organizations never really move past that first transaction. They just keep doing the first date over and over again (mostly with solicitations that keep asking, and asking, and asking). They continue to treat this "new" donor as if they enjoy their time with them solely for the transaction. And sadly, it's true.

The fact is, you can raise a lot of funds quickly through a transactional approach. The problem is, you have to keep asking, because the per-person gift amount is smaller. So you get more and more people on the email list. This list may be huge, but many of the contacts who are on it are no longer interested—or they say, "I've had enough," and they break up with you. Most won't break up officially— they just stop showing up. You might call once you've taken notice, but they lost interest long before you noticed.

When I build a relationship, I automatically make the assumption that the other person wants to form a relationship with me. It has to go both ways. Leave that decision to them, and to God. Remember, He is always at work. If you're shutting down relationships, you will miss out on what He's doing. Sometimes, it won't make sense—that's where we have to trust Him, and His ways.

For example, I have had experiences with others, internally and externally, with whom I disagree with on certain levels; but God, in His infinite wisdom, has managed to develop some great friendships from these experiences. Because I want to connect them to their passion-match,

I've been able to help many find their purpose, and move on. What was my return? A deepening trust of God. The joy of watching them blossom. And of course, their enduring friendship.

Without an agenda beyond simply adding value to them, I was given a tremendous return that could have only been orchestrated by the Lord.

Tune into His process, and trust it. It will move you forward.

FIVE

IT'S ALL ABOUT A RELATIONSHIP

n the previous chapter, I mentioned that we would address our internal relationships more specifically here. You might be wondering why I would be talking about internal relationships when this book is about building relationships with potential and current investors. If you do not have an internal relational culture that adds value to your associates, however, you will struggle to add that level of relational value externally. Just like you have to work on your personal values and character before you can impact others in a positive way, you also need to work on the values and character of your non-profit before you can effectively be relational externally.

Permit me to reiterate a few points before diving into the deep end.

If you're intentional about being relational, you may still find yourself prioritizing along the way and "hiccupping" on whether you are viewing and treating people equally. This is especially true when our attention is divided between our internal and external relationships. To put your mind at ease, I just want to remind you that it's your responsibility to be accountable to value people and add value to others first. If we value people internally, it will show up externally. God knows what we need and when we need it. He is responsible for supplying those needs, and as relational leaders, our responsibility is to be accountable and value people first. If we value everyone equally, we can leave the rest to God.

I define *excellence* as doing my very best with the resources, talent, and skills that I have been given. If you accept that definition, then you are accountable for one-hundred percent of whatever your role is in your non-profit. You are accountable to see that your associates have the resources they need to succeed, and you are responsible for providing the culture they need to grow in their skills, talents, and passions. As a person in a relational non-profit, you are accountable and responsible for the encouragement they need to work well, and to lead the celebration when a job is done well. You are responsible when some corrective action needs to be made. This is an example of why operating in the twenty percent will make a big difference. It's a mind-set and actions that will set your non-profit apart from the others.

Excellence should be your focus and top priority. Why? Because when your associates do their work with excellence, it will not only show up in the outcomes, but will also build stronger relationships with them. This will extend externally as well.

The only way to grow an organization is by training the people in your organization—developing them to be all they can be, empowering them in that training, and yes, even funding their mistakes. They make the eighty percent happen, as long as you are focused on the twenty percent, that makes your non-profit different.

In a true relationship, each party is intent on making the other person better by taking the time to help them fulfill their purpose. A perfect relationship is between two like-minded people who enjoy each other and feel like they can be themselves.

For those in the faith-based world, our approach to having all the resources we need is a mirrored response of our personal relationship with our heavenly Father. The closer we are to Him, the better we can relate to the people who come across our path and leave the rest up to Him.

If you are not a faith-based organization, being re-sourced starts with those whose job focuses squarely on engagement. They need to keep checking their pulse for pure motives and a mindset that is different from the norm of "get the check." As the Bible puts it, "with clean hands and a pure heart"—you have no ulterior motive but to add value to people. If it's anything but to enrich a person's life, we'd better not go any further in the relationship.

CREATING A RELATIONAL
CULTURE WITH ASSOCIATES

Leaders are to serve others, set an example, and add value to people. If you're a person of faith, this is a man-date. This is the biblical chain of command, and Christ sits at the top of the organizational chart. If you're not a person of faith, then you don't have a biblical chain of command. You're the boss, or the board of directors is the collective boss of your organization. The latter is much easier, in one sense; but in another, it's much harder because you don't have the benefits that come with being a person of faith—namely, the example set by Jesus that was recorded in scripture.

When we are focused on being more relational leaders, one of the quickest, most effective ways to connect with your associates is to look for occasions to thank them. Now I'm not talking about flowers and candy; I'm talking about those moments that occur on a daily basis where a simple thank-you is what they need to hear. If you enter a room and see two or three huddled and making things happen, call 'em out—thank them for their efforts! Let them know that you see them, see what they're doing, and that you're grateful for the effort they are putting in.

I have a team member who loves to do what she calls "field trips." We don't do them all that often, but after three, four, or five wins—things the team has done well—we'll take a field trip to a coffee shop and I'll buy them all their favorite coffee, or we'll do something out of the norm. Sometimes, we'll bring lunch in and celebrate. And everyone will look at each other at the associates' roundtable and say, "What are we celebrating?" It's no one's birthday, we're just celebrating some sort of win, like a new project that kicked off with excellence.

It's those little things that become memorable moments. You don't need to spend a lot of money and a lot of time on it. But there are two ways this can derail, and they both involve taking it a bit too far.

There was a time when I celebrated *all* the wins, and it didn't work. Why? The celebrations lost their value.

Every day I was throwing a party for something positive that somebody was doing. And pretty soon, it got to be a game they were playing. They were all trying to do some positives so we could get more parties. And there was no end to that—until, as the leader, I put a stop to it. You want the celebrations to mean something, have value, and be a little unpredictable. There are other ways to fill in the gaps between celebrations: A personal acknowledgement or simple thank you lets the individual or team know that their efforts have been seen. Expressing gratitude for who they are and how well they work together adds value.

Now the other way this can quickly derail is when you infringe on personal time by rewarding someone or a team with really nice dinners, or even a trip somewhere. Short work retreats are fine, if that's part of your culture, but don't expect a glowing reception if you're rewarding them in ways that require them to spend more time away from home. I'm going to explain why leaders must respect personal boundaries later in the chapter.

RESOLVING CONFLICT RELATIONALLY

A big, big part of creating a relational culture involves how you handle conflict. As much as I would love to say a relational culture yields peace, love, and smooth sailing, the problem is, we're human beings working with other human beings; and it's that human part that ensures that the work environment can't always be sunshine and smiles. There will be conflict, and hopefully by being more relational, you are minimizing it—but it will still arise. So how you handle it can make or break your culture; it's where the rubber meets the road.

I believe when you see something that isn't up to standard, you talk about it in real time. You do not wait twelve months and bring it up in a performance review; they need to hear and see it in real-time. Why?

- First of all, they won't remember it.

- Secondly, they're way beyond it.

- Thirdly, you allowed it to take root and continue all that time. And that creates a massive problem.

If it's possible to eliminate annual reviews, do it. I know large organizations have to comply—whether it's in their bylaws, a legal issue, a policy, or somehow regulated. If this is your situation, I would encourage you to make sure there are no surprises in the reviews, because whatever has occurred throughout the year has been handled in real-time. So, it should be a situation where you're saying, "I have to do this because it's a compliance thing, so let's grab coffee and just get it over with." There should be no surprises for the person whose performance is being reviewed.

If we're being relational and adding value to someone, how do we handle conflict in a way that's respectful, but not sugar-coated?

Well, you have probably already guessed that I'm going to ask you to consider whether you are helping someone through an area, a flaw, or a behavior that they may not be aware of, or if they are, they don't consider it to be problematic. A common question I might ask them is, "Do you see it this way?"

For example, I may be reading an email or document that will be sent to our investors and I spot something that seems harsh or could be misconstrued. I might say to the person who drafted it, "Hey, as I read through it, this is what it came across to me as . . . do you see it this way?"

If I really value that person, I don't want to just correct them by telling them what they've done wrong. I want to help them see how they can do better. There's an educational piece, a teachable moment, to it. Believe it or not, they usually respond with, "I see where you're coming from. Now I see it the exact same way. I get it. And here's how I think we can correct it."

Or, "Yeah, I think you're right. I think we need to . . . " And you just take the conversation from there, and move forward. Not that I have to be an expert in what they do (if I was, I wouldn't need them). It's not that at all, it's just about inspiring that person to go to the next level.

More recently, I had a situation where someone put something in an email that was inappropriate. I went to the sender and asked, "Could you help me understand why you sent this email?" This person thought they were being nice and embracing the relational mindset. So, I listened—*truly listened*, instead of thinking about what I was going to say next—and then explained to them how it was perceived by the recipient. I wanted to add value to the person without discouraging their efforts to be relational; I didn't want to scold the person who sent the email. I wanted them to learn from it, not be disciplined by it.

Sometimes, being relational includes some fine-tuning and this was one of those occasions. The sender didn't realize how the email had been received, and they will do better moving forward. As a result, they will rise to a higher level.

As chief stewards in our non-profits, when we see something that isn't appropriate, we need to consider a few things:

1. Do we really need to 'wait until the dust settles' to address it?

2. When our own emotions are attached to it— is this truly *wrong*, or is this more of a personal preference?

Unless you're about to lose your temper, I'm not sure there is any benefit to waiting—so that eliminates the first question.

That leaves us with the second question and your approach is contingent on your answer. If it's a preference, we take one approach. If it's really wrong, then deal with it straight-up and speak with the associate, like, "I think wearing slippers to work is really inappropriate. Is there a reason why you wore slippers to work for the last three days?" There may actually be a valid reason—like they had a cyst or a wart removed, and they are embarrassed about it. If I have already made up my mind and am not listening to their response, but instead crafting my own response to them in my head, I may miss something vital that explains the behavior.

Nor do I come at it like, "Stop wearing slippers now!" without giving them an opportunity to explain. Always provide them the trust and the freedom necessary to present their perspective.

Sometimes, conflicts arise internally because of external forces—in other words, when something outside the organization takes issue with something inside. This presents another opportunity to build trust. Part of relationship-building and trust-building among your associates happens when they realize how much you support them. There are those times when you will have to decide whether to acquiesce with someone "important" or with your associates, who are equally important. Since we're valuing all people the same, how is this done? I can illustrate it best through an example I learned about.

A number of years back, a non-profit had a wonderful investor who provided for them -every month without fail. But that investment was always accompanied by a letter containing all the ways they messed up during the previous month, all the things they didn't like about them, etc.

To say that the letters became annoying would be an understatement. In fact, the letters were demoralizing; it was their way of letting the organization know they couldn't do anything right. None of those letters ever mentioned even one positive item—not one single time. Do not let this kind of thing go on too long – this non-profit did and it went on—five, maybe six months. Finally, I suggested that the chief steward just make an appointment to go and see the person.

He told the person, "Your investment is valuable to us, because it comes with your prayers. You are extremely important to us in our mission." Then he asked questions to find out why the person was acting this way. After the conversation, he had to make a decision based on the discussion, so he swallowed hard and said something like: "I cannot keep taking this financial investment from you when it's accompanied by this kind of a letter. It is demoralizing to our associates. It's just not right. The way it's written isn't constructive—the tone, the way it's taken. But now that I know why you have written these letters, I think you should use this investment for the local mission you are passionate about." They got very upset, angry and didn't take it well at all. Truly, the upshot of that conversation was that they parted ways. Even though that was an uncomfortable discussion, it was the right thing to do. While hoping and praying for a better outcome, he stood by his associates and the work they were all doing . The associates knew that he would not stand for them to be treated that way. They knew he supported them, through and through. Incidentally, the investor also did what was suggested and got involved in a local mission.

So, we've talked about when something is truly wrong, or when conflict comes into the organization from external sources. But what happens if the conflict involves a personal preference? That's a whole different situation.

In fact, that's where I have to take a deep breath and probably talk to some other people—not to take a poll, but rather to speak with a very small group of trusted advisors. I need to hear, objectively, if this is something I should address, or is it just something I don't like.

The answer is not always either/or. Sometimes, it *is* a preference, but still needs to be addressed. When that happens, my approach is usually, "In all honesty, this is a preference that I'm going to talk to you about. From my viewpoint, I think _____ is wrong, and I'd like to talk to you about it." Be selective about these sorts of things, because you are asking for a change based on a preference; if the behavior itself is not wrong and doesn't violate any sort of policy, you need to recognize that in your discussion.

Preferences can get us into deep trouble, especially because my preferences are built on the lens that I look through: my faith and many years of experience. Sometimes, I have to let it go. Like certain clothing, hairstyles, or accessories; I have to remind myself that these are fads that will be gone within three years, so why am I spending time on that? There are bigger and more important issues that need my time and energy. If it doesn't harm the organization's integrity, let it go.

As you work intentionally and diligently to move your associates and your organization to a relational DNA, there are some general ways you can encourage them individually and collectively to capture the vision. Little things, like how an inbound call is handled, for example, add up to a whole lot of contributing factors. An answering device is a dead giveaway of the type of non-profit you are. In a relational organization, if you have a live human answer the phone—whether it's a designated receptionist or any associate who is available to answer—that is sign number one that you have a relational culture. If someone answers the phone and realizes they're not the right person to handle it, we need to teach them not to dismiss the caller; we stay friendly and helpful. We tell our associates not to defend themselves (i.e., "this isn't my job/you've landed in the wrong department/someone else handles this sort of thing," etc.). We ask them to listen to the caller, be as friendly as they can be, and to make a connection to the correct person.

People cannot see a smile over the phone, but if they can *feel* a smile over the phone, that will make their day. If the caller is prepared for an argument, a smile through the phone can diffuse the situation into a calmer discussion. Understand that mistakes will be made as your associates try to be more relational in their work, and have patience with them when mistakes happen, they are learning.

But what about those associates who simply can't get on board with the idea of being relational?

You have to find another place for them to use their gifts and talents. And I don't think that's a bad thing. This is different from someone who needs additional training or a better learning curve; I'm talking about someone who simply refuses to "get it."

I am very slow to hire and I am very fast to fire. When I was in the hiring process, it took a lot of time to make sure the applicant was the right fit. We did assessments, and all kinds of things to make sure that person was the best fit for the position. Sometimes, we'd ask someone from a different department to take a candidate to lunch to see how relational they were.

We do people a disservice by keeping them in positions that are not the right fit, thinking it's going to work out someday. You're not helping that person fulfill their mission in life, and you're not helping you fulfill *your* mission in life. So why are we putting up with the pain of this? Remember, it's *relational* to care more about the person and their purpose than trying to fit them into *my* purpose.

WHEN IT'S *YOUR* BLIND SPOT

This may be among the biggest tests to your relational mindset, because it squares off directly with your ego and requires a mind-shift on what it means to be the chief steward. When the blind spots are our own, how do we, as leaders, receive that information and respond in a way that helps *us* rise to a higher level?

Remember when I mentioned several chapters ago that you will always need to look inward and face some painful truths about yourself? That exercise is not one and done. If you're intentional about being relational and creating a relational culture in a relational organization, then you will persist in your humility. Sometimes, that means being brave enough to handle hearing about some of your own shortcomings from others.

For better or worse, your leadership style will emerge based on how you handle this, so read the rest of this section very carefully.

In relationships, you do not need to be right all of the time. When you are wrong, admit it, and take ownership of it without excuses. If the other person has done something wrong, forgive quickly and consider that maybe you misunderstood them. The real character test is not about figuring out who is right or wrong, but rather about taking responsibility for your actions—that's at the core of healthy and productive relationships.

So, if you make a mistake, own it. If you treat someone poorly, ask forgiveness. Getting defensive, making excuses, or blowing off steam never makes a relationship better. You might be one-hundred percent right, but why do you need to win? You just might lose in the long run.

When you are wronged, forgive quickly. You'll live with less stress and enjoy life more. When building a relationship, work on giving more than you take away—always. There may be a few people in your life that you think it's impossible to out-give, but with the majority of people that you will come in contact with, you can give more than you take.

This part reaches way beyond your mind and reveals your heart: If you are keeping score, you have missed the point. *This is not about keeping score*. When your motives are pure, and only when they're pure, will you receive great joy.

Transparency in communication must work both ways. Leaders must effectively manage and reassure associates that they will be heard without penalty—no psychological or passive-aggressive punishment when someone has a complaint or wants something changed. As chief stewardship officers, we have to learn to overcome our fear of criticism and rejection; we *will* be criticized, especially if it's something new we are implementing.

When the blind spot is the leader's, it's scary business for the associate. Most of us have either been in, or seen, situations where someone is told to be transparent, be open, and it won't be held against them. And then psychologically, that person gets penalized for complaining or raising an issue with the leader. Put yourself in their shoes for a moment. Whether their concerns have merit—and assume that they do—consider the courage it has taken this person to come forward and be honest.

Keep yourself in check during these moments. If you're sincere about having a relational culture, then you have already decided that psychological warfare creates a hostile environment, the kind that forces people out. No one enjoys criticism, but we want to add value to people— and you can't do that if you're taking your hurt feelings out on them.

Your associates have seen you work for years as a values-based leader. Trust is significant on both sides of the table, and trust does not mean they cannot criticize or express their concerns. Value-based leadership is foundational to handling the criticism that comes from both directions. They know that when they come to you with an opposing point of view or some criticism that you will not jump all over them. They'll know they will not be penalized because historically, you have shown them that they are valued.

Trust is a big, big issue for the chief stewardship officer. If people don't trust you, you're not going to be able to move them forward. Trust buys you a lot of room for mistakes and errors. The chief stewardship officer has to make sure that the calling of building relationship is, in fact, a calling—deeply implanted inside of you—and it will always be greater than the criticism on the outside of you.

Look, regardless of whether someone's criticism has legs or not, you're going to be on the receiving end of it at some point. You're going to face rejection. I take rejection as a form of God's protection, and I take criticism for the value that it is—criticism that I should evaluate, think through, but don't obsess over. I'm experienced enough to know that if I do something brand-new, it's really only brand-new to me; it's not brand-new to history. And if I'm convinced something will succeed, and when it does, those same critics will then become your biggest cheerleaders.

When we have the privilege to enrich people and add value to them, we contribute something positive in their lives. This can be done with everyone you come in contact with. Adding value isn't a complex idea that requires grand strategies, gestures, and flow charts; sometimes, just being polite or saying thank-you can turn someone's day around. We have an opportunity to make their lives better.

It's as simple as a kind and encouraging word, and sometimes it involves having enough love and courage to have a tough and honest conversation. Remember, even in the toughest conversations, you can still offer a positive word and encouragement.

RESPECTING PERSONAL SPACE

Remember the friend who suggested I write this book? He suggested it because he felt I struck the right balance of being personable and professional. He liked my approach—simply put, I knew the difference between taking him to lunch and showing up at his house for dinner.

Ever notice how some leaders, even at large non-profits, don't understand why their associates don't want to go on all-expense-paid retreats or even just to lunch every day? They get their feelings hurt and harbor resentment that their employees don't appreciate how good they've got it. We all want our organizations to feel like family, but think about it—we have boundaries, even within our own families. Why do we expect less from those whom we work with?

Associates do not want to disappoint you, and you certainly want to create a work culture that's enjoyable for everyone. But that doesn't mean you infringe on their personal time.

Personal space is different for everyone, but every chief stewardship officer needs to have a guardrail of personal space—their own, their associates', and their investors'—especially in today's world where things can be judged, misrepresented, or misinterpreted. Whether you are single or married, boundaries need to be set on where, when, and how you meet. This goes for associates and investors alike—because we treat everyone equally, right?

For example, if I'm meeting someone one-on-one, I will never meet in their home; it has to be in a coffee shop or restaurant, and it needs to be during a normal meeting time and not at five in the morning. I try not to take appointments after six in the evening, it just creates too much mental strain on me.

You need to set some personal boundaries and respect the boundaries of others. When you have an authentic relationship with someone, you just feel where their boundaries lie, you can just sense it in your gut. Every now and then, the situation might be reversed; someone is wanting to meet with you and they don't recognize how inappropriate the request is with regard to your personal boundaries. If you're in a relationship with this person, and you care about the relationship, you'll need to find the courage to say, "I'm uncomfortable doing that, but I would be willing to _____ instead."

When it fits to do so, always have an alternative suggestion. It may be that they're unaware you promised your spouse you'd be home by 6:00 p.m., no matter what. It may be that they didn't know you have a standing appointment each Wednesday, or you ensure someone else is always in attendance because they are the opposite sex. In my entire career, if someone is tip-toeing into my personal boundaries and I raise a red flag, they have never abandoned me over it. I'm not rude about it, of course, but I do speak up. More often than not, I'm met with, "Oh my goodness, I didn't think about that. Yes, let's go with your plan."

When we have those parameters already in place, it makes things a lot less awkward and protects our personal integrity, which builds trust with the people around us—those closest to us and beyond. Even if they don't agree with the boundary that's in place, they respect that you do not allow anyone—not even them—the opportunity to cross it.

And frankly, personal boundaries give introverts time to mentally rest and prepare.

This chapter has devoted a lot of ink to address conflict resolution—how to address it with associates, how to handle criticism when we're the ones being criticized, differences between preferences and policies, etc. I want take a short detour on personal space to address an increasingly sensitive, and related, subject: When conflict arises from different ethnic, cultural, and religious backgrounds.

In today's world, we are much more aware of *how much more aware* we need to be on this subject. So how do we navigate conflict that arises from these differences? I have two steps I take—and if possible, I take them proactively to avoid potential conflict.

First, I do my best to learn about that ethnic group, or that culture, or that faith. There may be practices, traditions, or holidays, for example, that I might not understand.

Secondly, I try to put myself at the center of where that other person is at the moment. That's really difficult to do, but if I'm really trying to get to know them and understand where they're coming from, I've got to get out of my comfort zone. Maybe I will attend some of their cultural events or read some literature; regardless, if I value the person, then I must also value their cultural background and respect the space it occupies within them.

Be mindful that you may unintentionally encroach on someone in these areas, simply because you don't know what you don't know. When that happens, do not get defensive or suggest they "toughen up." This is a learning opportunity for you, and hopefully for them, too. They will trust you more if you give them a safe space to express what they're feeling.

By now you might also be wondering why we have taken a whole chapter talking about non-profit associates and the importance of being internally relational. After all, this is a book about having all the resources one needs to operate a non-profit. The answer is because a non-profit is either relational or it's not. There is no such thing as relational funding! Your non-profit has to have a DNA culture that breeds relationships. This is job one, and the largest part of our twenty percent.

At the end of the day, it's about encouragement. It's about empowerment. It's about providing education and motivation for your team members to go to that next level. For years, I've used that phrase: *Let's go to the next level.* And if you meet anyone who has worked with me for the past twenty-plus years, they would say, "I still haven't figured out what the next level is, but I've enjoyed the journey."

Relationships are like the engine in your car. Without proper maintenance, they will not function right.

•——————• ◦ ● ◦ •——————•

SIX

A WARNING TO NON-PROFITS,
FAITH-BASED AND SECULAR

M any years ago, there was a woman who visited a non-profit fairly frequently, and it was understood that she received extra-special treatment from the moment she entered the building until she exited. Only certain people were permitted to address her, while others were not allowed to even speak to this person. One day, someone else arrived about the same time, and I heard a supervisor mention to the first person that the second person wasn't very important, they didn't give as much to the organization. The woman replied, "What makes you think my gift is anything less than theirs?"

It was practically a modern-day retelling of The Widow's Mite account from the Bible. A couple of things struck me about this:-

- She could see that she received special treatment.

- She was upset enough to speak up about it.

- She was totally right.

Even if it hadn't been obvious, this woman could sense she was receiving special treatment not because of who she was as a person, as a human being, but because of the amount of money she had given. Her value was based on that dollar amount—confirmed by the supervisor's remark—and her trust in the ministry deteriorated.

Following that incident, the relationship was damaged. I don't think it fell apart completely, but it certainly put some layers of distrust in there that maybe hadn't been there before. She instantly knew that the organization did not value her as a person and certainly did not seek to add value to her.

In the faith-based world, the person who gives the least might give the most, because it might be all they have. It might be five dollars, or it might be five million. And for some, that five million may be pocket change, whereas the person giving five dollars might be sacrificing part of their grocery budget for the week—and they're willing to eat a little less to help your mission, because they believe in what you are doing. We'll treat the former like they're royalty; why? Their gifts, while much appreciated, may not hold the same value from God's perspective. So why are we showing favor?

We should treat all people the same because we want to add value to them. How dare any of us say that one person holds more value than another? We are warned not to go there—and from a faith-based perspective, it's a command.

WARNING, OR SUGGESTION?

You may be thinking, "Tom, using the word *warning* is a bit harsh. This is just how it is—why shouldn't we pay more attention to those whose gifts are larger? We don't want to lose *their* favor." Let's see what James had to say about the Lord's warning:

> *For if there come unto your assembly a man with a gold ring, in goodly apparel, and there come in also a poor man in vile raiment;*
> *And ye have respect to him that weareth the gay clothing, and say unto him, Sit thou here in a good place; and say to the poor, Stand thou there, or sit here under my footstool:*
> *Are ye not then partial in yourselves, and are become judges of evil thoughts?*
> (James 2:3–4, KJV)

Now if your Early Modern English is about as rusty as mine, here is my paraphrase of the passage above: Do not show favoritism, do not show partiality—it's a very strong warning. *Don't do this.*

This is a clear warning, from the writings of the biological brother of Jesus, who didn't come to faith until after the resurrection. Throughout his lifetime, James bore witness to the negative effects of favoritism. And when he saw it after he was a follower of his brother's, it just blew his mind. It blew every circuit in his thinking. No matter the translation or paraphrase, it still comes out the same: *Do not.* It's a warning, not a suggestion, and should be treated as such.

Once we are followers of Jesus Christ, we do not want to get the idea that we are the only one God needs; if you are genuinely concerned for people, you will treat people equally. The sin of partiality brings death to the interpersonal relationship—something that could have been meaningful, and could have served as a bridge to introducing a person to eternal life through faith in Jesus Christ. Your lack of integrity is displayed when you play favorites. We love our group, our circle, our tribe; and of course, it's easier to reside there, living in our comfort zone. When someone new wants to join, it upsets the herd—so we tend to push back to where we are comfortable, at ease, and settled. Where does 'love thy neighbor' fit into this attitude?

James and Jesus himself are very clear about this, but if your organization isn't faith-based, you're not exactly off the hook. When you start playing favorites with people, you'll never end up in a good place. Be wise to this warning; yes, it's a directive from a faith-based standpoint, but once you start separating the gives from the give-nots, or the big-gives from the little-gives, you're landing right back into a transactional mindset that will not accomplish what you intend for segmentation to do. Value people, value your fellow human beings. I don't want to sound preachy, but this is still the right thing to do and the right path to take, regardless of whether your organization is faith-based or not.

If we are intentional about being relational, all people should have the same value to us because they are people of value. We get into trouble when we get into this whole area of segmentation of our investor base, based on dollar amounts. Pay attention to this next part, because this is where your marketing department really has to get on board with being relational.

When we segment, it should be based on the person's passion, first. Then as you communicate with them, everyone needs to receive a story that matches their passion. Stories are key, and each story must paint the picture of not only what they invested in, but also the return that was provided. Fact-filled email and/or letter communications do not paint a personal story. Stories are remembered, but facts fade. Do not give people facts— instead, tell them a factual story that *illustrates* the facts! Do not tell them what you do, share a story with them that shows what you do. Seek to connect their passion to an area of your organization that you're passionate about.

I'm saying we must segment, but we need to do it much more strategically. We need to be stewards, not salespeople. We must add value to the investor by not throwing everyone into the same kettle. Would it not be better to segment based on their passion instead of on dollar amounts?

The only way to segment according to passion-matches is by developing a relationship with that person and stewarding that relationship. The segmentation occurs as the relationship develops. You're looking at their motivation and passion to why they gave—not about how many dollars they gave.

True segmentations can occur after you've viewed, met the passion need, and met the motivation. *Then* you might sub-categorize based on your dollar amount, because your list is so big. This is the road usually *not* taken, and this is living in the twenty percent.

Segmentation based on dollar amounts is the easier path and it's a single criterion. Motivations, passion-matches, and relationships are messy and detailed, but you can be sure the recipient knows that you 'get' them and thereby are adding value to them.

So, here's a question regarding the crossover between motivation and passion: Does passion drive their motivation, or does their motivation drive their passion? At the end of the day, it is impossible for us to judge one's motives. We can see what they are doing, but *why* they are they doing it, is really impossible for us to know.

CARING IS A CUSTOM JOB

Regardless, followers of Jesus Christ cannot be partial to either the rich or the poor. The poor are "obvious," in the sense that their immediate needs are often physical and therefore, more recognizable. But why should we also care for the wealthy—can't they afford whatever they want or need?

We don't usually think about the rich having needs—they are supposed to help, right? In my experience, I have often found that the rich actually have *more* complicated needs than those living in poverty.

Most people living in poverty have more motivation, more excitement, more hope and are willing to learn, change, and grow. Whereas the rich, on the other hand, are lonely and sometimes struggle with depression. This is difficult for them to admit; pride and arrogance get in the way, when they actually need a shoulder to cry on, an arm to hug them, and someone who truly cares about *them*— not their bank account.

Now, pay careful attention to this next part, because it's going to seem as though I'm contradicting myself—but I think the people who treat the wealthy the exact same as the poor are just lazy. Stay with me here.

You should pay as much attention to the wealthy as you do the poor, but *how* you pay attention will be different. Instead of giving them a bag of food, like we would for someone who is hungry, you might engage in an uplifting, encouraging conversation. Or send them a book on something that might interest them, along with a little note saying, 'Hey, this book was meaningful to me. I hope it's meaningful to you.'

It's much easier to say, "Everyone below this threshold gets a receipt. Everyone above this line gets a receipt and a thank-you gift. And everybody above the next division line gets a receipt, thank-you gift, and a personal visit. It's also much easier to say, "If someone gives X amount, then we will give them Y. If someone gives Z amount, their receipt will serve as an acknowledgement, but they don't get Y." It's much harder to personalize these, and take the time to have conversations that identify individual needs.

The ministry that I cofounded serves about 4,000 families per month who are living at or below the poverty line. Every six months an assessment is conducted with each family to find out what they really need—we literally sit down with them and have a conversation. While there, the team looks around for unspoken needs—usually, the family lives in a tent near a farmer's field—and make a note of what's on the shelf, because there's likely only one shelf and no kitchen. They might have a little one-burner gas stove, one mattress, one pillow. So they likely don't need an excess amount of food because it will rot or go to waste; but they have six children, so they could use more mattresses and pillows. And that's what we'll provide, along with, hopefully, a better night's sleep.

Identifying needs has to be done on an individual level, and that takes a lot of time for the associates and administration. The other way is much easier—but you're not really meeting needs, you're just checking your own boxes.

If we value people, why would we treat everyone exactly the same? There is a difference between how we regard people and the way in which that regard will manifest. In other words, we are to value people exactly the same, but how we demonstrate or add value will be different, down to the individual level. Relationships are messy and highly customizable. As we take the time and effort to get to know someone, we learn their quirks, preferences, motivations, fears . . . and there's not a 'one-size-fits-all' way to add value to a person, beyond taking the time to steward a true relationship that's built on trust instead of dollar amounts, or what we might gain (clout, power, visibility, status, etc.). Many organizations take this approach, preferring to stay disconnected from those who support them and those whom they serve.

We should want to add value to the poor as much as we want to add value to the wealthy. If we are relational, we will regard them the same, but how we care for them and develop the relationships will be different and very individualized. And that takes work.

Being relational is not modular; this attitude should be in our DNA. It has to be a part of who we are, our philosophy, and our belief system. The conversations you have let you deal with more than just their physical needs; you have an opportunity to deal with their emotional and psychological needs, too.

If you're from the faith-based world, the conversations will likely lead to understanding their spiritual needs, so I do want to make one thing clear: You do not enter these conversations with that agenda. This is particularly important if your organization is a ministry. That seems counterintuitive—but if you have any agenda of your own, besides adding value to the person, you're not being relational. As believers, however, be aware that spiritual needs will likely surface in those conversations, and what a remarkable opportunity and privilege it is to share our hope in the eternal with someone else.

THE LAW OF RECIPROCITY

We have to love people first, as Christ loved us. With open hands and clean hearts, we need to accept people the way they are, and be sensitive not only to the spirit of

God, to the word of God, but also to the *people* of God. He places people in our path for a reason. And in the scripture verses I mentioned earlier, James is saying a genuine Christian is one who has a real concern for people.

You see, God is in the people business and therefore, so are those of us who follow Jesus. So how do we do this? James 2:8 gives us the answer: *love.*

Everyone comes into our lives at the same level of relationship opportunity—and we should be mindful of this. When you love others with Christ's love, you are always at eye-level with others. Christ loves them all, and so should we. Believers should be the most open and greatest social group of all people, where everyone is treated equally. Galatians 3:28 is very clear, we are to show no favoritism, no partiality! None, zero.

So, this is where I really want us to re-think the term *fundraiser*. I have such a distaste for that word. As relational people and relational organizations, we are not fundraisers.

- If you believe, like I do, that raising funds is God's responsibility, then we are not fundraisers.

- If you believe, like I do, that fundraising is transactional—then we are not fundraisers.

- If you believe, like I do, that we have a higher calling than raising funds, then we are not fundraisers.

If I am to have a title, a tag, and a label for my role in a relational organization, I want one that goes to the heart of who I am, indicates where my heart is, and reflects what

I want to accomplish. That's why I consider myself to be an *engagement specialist*. You are welcome to borrow my title, or you may think of another one that fits the same criteria.

We are called to engage people with the work God is doing in the area that they are passionate about. We connect people's passion to a mission where they can be blessed and rewarded accordingly.

A lot of leadership programs reinforce the Law of Reciprocity, which states that when someone does something nice for you (adds value), you will have a deep-rooted, psychological urge to do something nice (add value) to them in return. In many cases, one might reciprocate with a greater gesture, which is far more generous than the original good deed. Does this law apply in a relational organization? How?

Yes and no (how's that for a definitive answer?).

Yes, the Law of Reciprocity trues up when we are relational—but no, not in the way you think, or in the way you have seen it play out before.

Relational people in relational organizations are hopeful about developing relationships with those they encounter; they seek to add value to those individuals. If a true relationship forms, the care and concern is reciprocated—but we're not focused on what they can do for us. I think it's important to have an awareness of the Law of Reciprocity and trust in its promise, but if it becomes our end-game, we have lost our focus. In fact, if it becomes a game at all, we have lost our focus.

Every investor knows non-profits need funding, and most are suspect of a person who is more interested in them than in their money—and for good reason. In their mind, they're waiting for the shoe to drop. In anticipation, they're wondering, "When is the ask coming? Is this for real, do they really care?"

This mental back and forth creates several points of tension:

- The length of time and money you spend to get the first investment

- When it's really all about the person, and not the financial investment

- The investor's passion and the organization's needs

Tension is good, if it's managed well, because it has the potential to make everyone involved better. You are accountable for the tension in a relationship with the investor.

The difference between managing your relationship and playing the fundraising game requires a persistent self-check of your own motives. If you're not careful, you can play a fundraising game with some of the activities your organization might host. Not that there is anything wrong with a golf tournament or a skeet shoot, but if you think that's relationship-building, you are sadly mistaken. Those are fundraising events, and they are transactional.

That's playing a game, even with only a soft ask. You're not being relational. The difference? If you're in a genuine relationship, you would say, "Hey, I'm going to go play golf tomorrow. Come with me as my guest." Over time, if you are truly relational, they will get it—relationships win the day.

Let me provide an example from my own experience. On August 4, 2020, the world's second-largest explosion took place in the port of Beirut, Lebanon. According to the BBC, "Based on an analysis of videos, a team from the University of Sheffield estimated that the explosion was the equivalent of 1,000 to 1,500 tons of TNT—about a 10th of the intensity of the nuclear bomb dropped on Hiroshima in 1945." It killed a reported 154 people, wounded more than 5,000, and caused widespread damage. Over 3,000 families were displaced. More than 1,000 people were hospitalized, with 120 in critical condition.

Heart for Lebanon (an NGO in Lebanon I co-founded) sprang into action within hours of the blast—and what surprised me were the people who called and said, "I just sent in *X* dollars, how is the team?" Or, "What do you need beside prayer? I'll send it today!"

Within a couple of weeks, we had just under a million dollars, and we never asked for a dime—nor did we send a fundraising email, make a fundraising phone call, or send a text.

It was the result of fourteen years of relationships that led to the enactment of the Law of Reciprocity.

Let me issue a very strong warning here: *Relational engagement is not a game you can or should play!* You build a relationship because you meet someone with a common interest with your organization, and you enjoy each other's company. Your motive is to enrich *them*—not the other way around. It's a mindset shift. This is why it takes a lot of work and time. And why many times a tension comes into play, and breaks the relationship.

WHEN LOVE IS . . . 'CHALLENGING'

I think it's important to address when love becomes a challenge. There are many reasons this occurs, but it does not let us off the hook—we are still accountable to how we manage and steward the challenges.

There is a difference between loving people and truly liking people. I am commanded to love others as God loves me. That is the gold standard. That's what we are to do. But our personalities, the way we're wired, the way we're built, the way we see life through the particular lens of our life experiences is what will attract us to certain people. And the truth is, it will repel us from others.

When we don't have a real passion-match, it doesn't mean that we de-value them. There is a reason they have come across our path, so we try to learn from them. Whether they're unpleasant, dishonest, or wherever the friction lies, we work with what we've got and do not shut them out; we keep the lines of communication open. I've lived long enough to know that it's not a good idea to burn bridges because when it's least expected, guess what? They will resurface.

We may never forget the pain from before, but if we have forgiving hearts, the details become foggier as time goes on. Make a conscious decision to contribute something positive to their story; whether they accept it or not, well, that isn't really your responsibility. But take responsibility to contribute something positive to their story—because if you think about it, we all have the opportunity to be active contributors to a greater story.

This is especially true when you have to have those difficult conversations. Put yourself on the offense; swallow hard and just say, "You know what, I'm sorry if what I said offended you, and you might not agree totally."

Stay open to communicating. Remember them in prayer. Don't pester or irritate the situation more, but maybe every once in a while, send an email that asks how they're doing. And if they don't respond, it's fine, be okay with that. When you feel this tension in your ministry, lean into it, manage it properly, learn from it, and move forward. When tension comes, don't back away from it—otherwise, you will stop moving forward and making yourself better. Running from tension is not taking the effort to find a better solution to the tension.

PARTING PASSIONS, PARTING WAYS, AND PARTNERSHIPS

There is an African proverb says, "Two can walk together further and faster than they can by themselves." It is so true!

You can't do everything and do everything well. Sometimes, someone needs assistance beyond your skillset, or their passions simply are not a match for yours.

As chief stewardship officer, you also have a relational responsibility to meet the investor's changing needs while not forsaking the organization or the cause. When an investor's needs have changed and your organization can no longer accommodate those needs, it is important to have partnerships with other organizations who could make use of what this person has to offer and what they are passionate about. After all, we still want to add value to them, so through partnerships, we can still help meet those needs.

One of my great frustrations in a partnership involves how I define a *true* partnership. To me, a partnership is when one is willing to give up one-hundred percent of their ego or as much of their ego as they can. "One-hundred percent" of someone's ego means finding someone else to do the task because they are better at it—they have the skill set, the training, the education, or certification, whatever it is. When it comes to helping someone find their passion-match, your ego should not be a part of this equation.

Our partners are organizations that do things better than we can in specific areas. For example, in the ministry I co-founded, we do not work with teenagers because there is a youth organization in the country of Lebanon that focuses on youth and their concentrated attention to this age group is more beneficial than for us to attempt it and spread ourselves too thin. Our values align with this organization, so we can direct investors and those with needs to them with full hearts; by the same arrangement, they can direct families and investors to us. Partnerships are messy, complicated, and confusing. But the results are far greater.

Your partnerships should be highly relational. Remember, your respective organizations are traveling in two separate lanes, but you support each other's mission in various ways. Trust is essential; ideally, they would say, "I have such a great relationship with you that I can totally, one-hundred percent trust you, because you're adding value to the families that we serve by taking care of a need."

The same warning we have for our individual relationships also applies to our partnerships: You want to add value to your contacts at that organization, and add value to the organization itself by serving them through your partnership.

VISIONARIES PLAN LONG-TERM GROWTH

Non-profits need to recognize that when we meet someone and interact with them a few times, we move into the beginning of what I call the "engage stage." This is the stage when relationships have the greatest potential to grow, but *you* will need to be intentional and take the initiative—not the investor. This is part of the twenty percent you're responsible for in the organization.

In a relationship, people invest; in a transaction, people are donors who give. If we are intent about forming a relationship, we focus on the long-term rather than the short-term; it's about the personal lifetime value rather than the short-term, or seasonal, transactional encounters. Relationships take a significant amount of time with a tremendous personal emphasis rather than very little non-personal/pleasantries type of emphasis. A relationship actually focuses on the *relationship*, not on the financial investment. You are growing together, and it's transformational—not transactional.

Transformation takes place when we have a value adjustment that is evident by the behavior-change we see. In 2009, Heart for Lebanon began teaching values to the children enrolled in their H.O.P.E. (Helping Overcome Poverty Through Education) Educational Program. The two-year curriculum focuses on twenty key values that affect their (our) character. For example, one of the values we teach is respect. As we worked through the curriculum with the children, we noticed a significant decline in bullying, and more mutual respect and cooperation on the playground. Their behavior did not just change (change modifies behavior), it was transformed. These are behavioral changes that will last a lifetime—later, respect will manifest in ways like husbands respecting their wives, or women respecting other women instead of putting them down. Respectful children become respectful adults.

When we make a change in our values, a transformation occurs that washes out the old and brings a new value into our being. We need to consider our relationship engagement as a value-change. This means non-profits need to give, or do more, to help investors find meaning in their lives by connecting them to their passions. This is a journey you, as a non-profit leader, must own; it's the journey your investors are on, and you need to take the initiative to connect with them on that platform.

Each investor I have met is on a focused quest to discover their purpose, and to live it out. What is thrilling is that we have the privilege to be a source of encouragement on this journey with them.

Earlier in this book, we discussed the difference between being relational and being friendly. Most fundraisers I know are not relational; many of them are, however, friendly. If you are intentional about making a value-change to be more relational, be aware that there is fine line that should never be crossed: Having a relationship with a person who may or may not become an investor does not mean you should disregard personal boundaries.

Your relationship is built on engagement, but this does not mean you push yourself into their personal lives (or they into yours). In fact, pushiness has no place here; there are no deadlines or benchmarks if you're organically and sincerely building a relationship. The engagement we are talking about here cannot be accurately communicated through bar graphs, spreadsheets, or some other measurement tool; remember, you are making an investment with them, too. Initiate contact, yes—but not so you can check a box on your to-do list, or because you looked at the coffers this morning, and they are low. By the same token, you do not need to tell them about an argument you had with your spouse, or press them for details about their personal lives when they've made it clear they don't want to.

The best relational people in the non-profit world I know are engagement specialists. They engage the investor in their passion—that is the goal, to connect one to the other. They are not concerned with asking for and getting money; they are more visionary than this, thinking beyond the present and more into the future. In reality, they are always one to three steps ahead of others. They care about the investor personally, pray for them, and help them when invited in to do so.

Over the last few years, research has shown that 93 percent of donors will definitely or probably give again if you communicate with them more effectively; 64 percent would give even more. This is good information to file away, but put it through the lens of being relational—how can you *engage* with them more effectively? Everyone knows non-profits need money; let investors ask you when they are ready and in their own timing. A true relational person never thinks about asking for the investment, but using these statistics, are there other ways you can engage with investors and help connect them with their passions?

A STICKY RELATIONSHIP
IS A GOOD RELATIONSHIP

As I read numerous research reports, they show that more than half of investors *don't* receive the communication they need to stick with you. If you're relational, you will know how important this is. Remember, we are specialists in connecting them to their passion. So proper communication is key.

With all the technology we have today, it's unacceptable not to customize our communication to the investor; it's really not that difficult to give investors a transformative experience. Organizations and their boards need to commit to do a regular audit of their transformation process.

Now this next part is where I often lose marketing and development directors, but usually, it's only temporary: *Relational people do not want, nor do they read, mass emails.* Read that statement again. And again.

Mass emails are not even close to being relational. Investors might read a personal email, but a personal text or phone call from you has a far greater chance of being acknowledged. With this in mind, here are a few suggestions to have a transformative engagement mindset:

- You need to be prompt—thank them personally ASAP.

- You need to be personal—no 'form' letters— remember we are transforming them, engaging them to build a relationship with a *person*, not the organization.

- Personalize (or at least, segment) thank-you/receipt letters for different campaigns and different portfolios.

- You need different thank-you letters for different investment groups.

- You need to thank more than once when appropriate, preferably from different people.

Here are a few suggestions when engaging with the transforming investor:

- You need to always think from the investor's perspective.

- You need effective stories for the heart of your communications.

- You need to use Zoom or some other system to communicate with investors.

- You need to connect with investors frequently, and in person.

- Texting is the preferred way for most major investors.

Relationships change over time. They are developed, nurtured, and cultivated. Much like dating, you have a few polite, cordial dates that move to more familiarity. As your bond deepens, you move to engagement. And now, you are working together to accomplish the passion of both parties.

At the start of a relationship, people are attracted to the cause or organization because of the good work it does, and how it helps its beneficiaries. In my own experience—and, based on research, the experiences of others—it is clear that once that initial stage has come to pass and as you grow in your relationship with each other, their focus changes. They are concerned much more about what the relationship delivers for them, and much less about what it delivers for the non-profit relationship partner.

Soon, the relationship is more about the two individuals—the investor and his/her organization's contact—than with the organization itself. This is why your communication is so important; the investor will be more satisfied with any relationship they have with a charity if they feel the charity is meeting their needs (rather than the needs of the mission beneficiary). You may not like this, but it's what the theory unequivocally tells us is the case.

Along those lines, is there a litmus test to determine when an email, a phone call, an actual letter, or even an in-person visit is appropriate? What should be your guidelines? As chief stewardship officer, you need to think through what's appropriate based on what you know about this person so far, and how much you value people. For example, in one of the organizations I led, I was in charge of daily operations; during that time, anyone who made a financial investment received a live phone call to thank them within twenty-four hours of receipt.

It was someone's full-time job to make those calls. In fact, I also made hundreds of calls. We kept adding associates and volunteers to make this happen. We believed this personal touch, in a timely manner, was a good way to steward these relationships. It was not a way to raise more money or get a second investment.

You have to figure out what's valuable to you and the organization. What is a value that makes you part of the twenty percent? What makes you different, distinct? I can tell you one that will make your non-profit different—find a unique, sincere way to simply say, *thank you*. That's part of the twenty percent. In our case, I just picked up the phone, knowing that 94 percent of the phone calls were going to voicemail. A voicemail, however, can be just as encouraging. And depending on the person, that phone call is as good as a one-on-one in-person meeting—just hearing from someone they know, when they pick up the phone. Don't look at this as like, *Well, nobody's going to answer, why am I calling them?* The heart of the matter *is* the heart of the matter. Most non-profits thank people with just a receipt; be different, swim in the twenty percent, and find a way to express your thanks that is meaningful to the investor. You want your relationship to be "sticky," in the sense that they will stick with you.

God brings people into our paths—never forget that, especially when someone is particularly difficult or appears to have nothing in common with us. Our responsibility is to have conversations and build relationships so that when there is a passion-match, we can fill it—or when tension arises, we can learn from it. Every person has value, and we are warned against thinking otherwise.

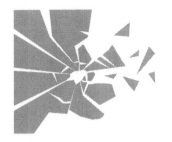

SEVEN

EVERYONE KNOWS IT, SO WHY ARE YOU TALKING ABOUT IT?

Back in the early 1980s, I had an opportunity to sit in a meeting with Dr. Charles Stanley, along with other full-time Christian workers. A few hours later, I found myself at Dr. Stanley's roundtable for lunch, as did eight other faith-based leaders.

After some conversation from those present, the conversation turned from how their church attendance was down to offerings being lower, too. Dr. Stanley said, "Gentlemen, your job is to be accountable; it's God's responsibility for the outcome."

You could have heard a pin drop.

It was a lightbulb moment for me. *Of course God is responsible.* If He called us to do the work, He will be faithful not only in knowing *what* we need, but *providing* it.

I proceeded to study this principle, and shortly thereafter, accepted this as a principle I would operate under. I would strive to live my entire earthly life this way. Looking back, it has taken the pressure off one area, but added tremendous pressure in terms of accountability.

At times, I might have taken this too far; if I've been offered a job, I have never asked, "What's the pay?" In every case, however, when I was paid, it was more than I would have asked for. Understanding God's responsibility and focusing solely on my own responsibility has enabled me to fully experience the joy that comes with adding value to others and watch The Law of Reciprocity take place—that's something so priceless, I can't even express how precious and valuable it has been.

As I have walked with this core philosophic pillar of being 'accountable, but not responsible,' I have come to terms with its actual heavy, full-time responsibility. It's not only a daily sense of responsibility—it's moment-by-moment.

We are responsible for one thing: to be accountable for all aspects of our lives and ministry. This includes adding value to people. If you raise funds for your non-profit, stop for a moment and consider if you value people *first*, and hold yourself accountable for that.

Look, we all know that every non-profit in the world needs funding—so why are we talking about it?

Before we walk down this path, let's look at some history on how God provided.

MÜLLER, TAYLOR, AND MOODY

When I think of engagement specialists in post-biblical times , three heroes of the faith come to mind: George Müller, Hudson Taylor, both from England, and D.L. Moody from the United States. These three men have been the role models that many of us have built our modern-day ministry philosophy around.

George Müller was a former lawyer turned prolific preacher. He had a passion for orphans and began numerous orphanages throughout London. Müller trusted in God deeply, even with the finances he needed, and took Him at His word. During the final forty years of his life, he spent time in prayer and told that same story every night to overflow crowds in cities all over the world. In fact, that's all he did—he prayed, told stories, and trusted his Heavenly Father with the rest.

He estimated that he had read the Bible cover-to-cover approximately two hundred times over the course of his life, with half of those times on his knees. George Müller learned and believed that God could do more than man, so he told God his needs and believed God would supply them.

Müller kept a notebook with two columns. In one column he gave the petition and the date; in the opposite column, he entered the date of the specific answer. Thus, there was no guesswork as to when God answers his prayers. Once, he was asked how many of his prayers God had answered, and he responded, "Five thousand, that I know of." At the end of George Müller's life, at least 50,000 of his prayers had been answered.

"The Lord pours in, while we seek to pour out," he explained.

George Müller was consistent throughout his life and never wavered in his belief that God had his ministry—he did not consider it his own, but rather, it was God's. He prayed, kept great records, reported with transparency and accountability, and told stories over and over again . . . but never asked for people to financially support his ministry. Yet the money poured in! Hold that thought, and let's shift to his friend Hudson Taylor.

Hudson Taylor was a young man when he began his own missionary career. Müller started the China Inland Mission Society in 1865, and it became very influential. If you read Müller's and Taylor's prayer journals, they are a lesson on faith and reveal that much of Taylor's funding actually came from excess donations that Müller passed on to him! Müller was a careful steward with God's provision, and by funding Hudson Taylor's work in China, he made quite an investment.

Taylor was the most widely successful missionary in China's history. During his fifty-one years there, China Inland Mission established twenty mission stations. By 1911, his mission brought nearly one thousand missionaries to the field, trained some seven hundred Chinese workers, raised four million dollars by faith (following Müller's example), and developed a Chinese church movement of 125,000 who were witnessing all over China. It has been said at least 35,000 were his own converts, and that he baptized some 50,000. His gift for inspiring people to give themselves and their resources to Christ was amazing.

Müller and Taylor never wavered; both sought God not only to supply for their own needs, but for God to pour in the funds and supplies the ministries needed. Because of God's blessing, both men diligently built specific strategies, procedures, and structures through which they could distribute aid and share the gospel with accountability and transparency.

Read this next part slowly: *Besides spending hours in prayer and building a deep relationship with their Heavenly Father, both men had an extremely high level of accountability and transparency within their ministry.*

- They both oversaw the careful distribution of money and supplies, measured everything, kept detailed records, and made them all public.

- They told stories of God's faithfulness and what those funds were accomplishing.

- They stopped short of what many do today—they never asked for financial support. They didn't have to; people were so moved by the stories these men told about how God moved and, in return, He never failed to bring in the funds needed, when they were needed.

D.L. Moody took a far different approach. A barely educated, mountain of a man, Moody went from selling shoes in Boston to being the world's leading and most well-known evangelist until Billy Graham came along. Today's sophisticated fundraising—complete with computers and direct mail, text, and all the rest—owes its roots to D.L. Moody. One of his sayings says it all: "Blessed are the money-raisers, for in heaven they shall stand next to the martyrs."

While Moody did an actual ask, he was known for personally writing hundreds of letters a day (there was no email back then). Other appeal letters were typed for him by the hundreds and occasionally, thousands, of volunteers—remember, there were no photocopy machines. Moody preferred to sign each letter personally rather than have his signature stamped. Modern fundraising definitely owes its roots to Moody, but his methods still included a personal touch.

Moody was also slightly suspicious that without an appeal, you had weak or no faith. Without an ask, your faith was one-sided. He did not understand the faith Müller or Taylor practiced; for Moody, faith meant doing *and* believing something. He said, "I show my faith when I go to men and state to them the needs of the Lord's work and ask them to give to it."

- Müller practiced minimal information and no solicitation.

- Taylor stood for full information and no solicitation.

- Moody stood for both full information and full solicitation.

Moody was not ashamed to ask people to invest big dollars in the Kingdom. He was often criticized for being too brazen, but he kept on asking, anyway. So, the question that comes to mind is: Why was D.L. Moody so different in his fundraising philosophy?

D.L. Moody was himself a businessman. In no way was Moody an average shoe salesman—he was an out-of-the-box thinker. He left home at an early age and moved to Boston and sold shoes at his uncle's store. He loved the interaction with people; he was excited to show and tell people about the shoes. Unlike the other salesmen who waited for customers to come into the store, Moody took to the streets, running after customers, selling them on the idea that they needed shoes. The shoes he sold, to be exact.

As he gained experience, Moody's wages and opportunities at the Boston shoe store seemed too small—he wanted more. With another uncle living in Chicago, D.L. Moody decided to move to Chicago in 1856. His uncle helped him secure a job in a local shoe store. Within a short time of his arrival, Moody had a goal to earn $100,000, and with some hard work and passion, his goal was within reach.

It was around this time that Moody started to take his Christian faith more seriously. He found himself dividing more of his time between selling shoes and his growing ministry at church. He sensed God calling him to devote all his talent and time to the work of reaching Chicago's children through Sunday School.

So, what was his primary talent? It was salesmanship—a passionate, persuasive, practical-focused-mind to sell, backed by abundant energy and an earnest heart.

Moody was a businessman/salesman who entered the gospel ministry—not a gospel minister who only later in life took on business ideas and practices. His background led him to a deep belief that it was highly honorable to raise money and ask for it, as long as the cause was worthy. Moody did not approach fundraising the way some of his contemporaries did, by fishing constantly and begging for funds. Nor did he promote what I call the "ouch system"— a technique where one keeps increasing the ask until the person says "ouch," and stops investing.

Let me bullet-point these three another way:

- George Müller prayed. Shared no information with no solicitation; was accountable, prolific story teller, but believed God would provide.

- Hudson Taylor prayed and shared needs. Kept great records, was an inspiring storyteller and reported on the ministry with accountability, but without financial solicitation.

- D.L. Moody prayed, shared needs, had high accountability, and asked. He was fully transparent with information on the ministry and in his solicitation and shared life transformational stories.

Notice that all three have two things in common: They all spent a tremendous amount of time in prayer. This is the first crucial part of the process of engagement. It's something that boards and investors need to spend more time in, and keep measuring. Not measuring the results of prayer with a formula; rather, how much are we praying, for whom, for what, and recording answers to prayer— not just for those as they relate to the organization, but for those directed at the people whom God places in our path. Second, all three were master storytellers. Their stories moved mountains.

By far the most powerful tool you have to build and deepen relationships with people is storytelling. Learn how to tell stories like these three men and you will have deep and lasting relationships.

THE PRAYER ARM OF AN ORGANIZATION

Any time I have had direct stewardship responsibility over a ministry, the very first thing I have done is put a prayer program in place. Personally, I believe it's the reason for the unprecedented increases in several ministries I led—not my own abilities, but the power of prayer. God did what God did in each ministry because of prayer. I won't spend too much time in this book focused on the importance of prayer, or why we should be involved in it personally and within our respective organizations; however, if I was a betting man, I would wager many of you could provide accounts on the measuring part of a prayer ministry.

Let's be very clear: The prayer ministry is *not* part of the development department. It is separate, because it's not about raising financial investments or engaging people into the ministry. You cannot measure its efficacy by how much money it brought in; if you do, it will cost you! It should be a ministry for all people who come in contact with your organization—it's a value question you must answer.

I am a very strong proponent of prayer ministries, because I value people and I know the value God places on people. I am also involved in a prayer ministry because of the power of prayer. In the previous chapter, I mentioned that I refer to myself as an engagement specialist. You may have thought, "Now Tom, isn't that just a fancy word for fundraiser? What's the difference?"

Fundraisers are responsible for raising the money, but engagement specialists are not. Engagement specialists are responsible for engaging others—associates, investors, namely—in their passions, whether it results in the bottom line of their organization or not. Engagement specialists want to go beyond any sort of financial gift—they want a passion-match for the other person. Ultimately, it would be nice to have investors involved as prayer partners or volunteers, but we really want their hearts moved and their itches scratched; we want to engage them at a heart and mind level, not just a pocketbook level.

Those of us who are engagement specialists understand the importance and the power of this. Prayer places us in direct contact with Almighty God, and we should expect almighty results. Whether or not He chooses to grant our petitions or deny our requests—that is His business, and we trust Him with the decision. Remember, *He* is responsible, and we are accountable. Whatever the answer to our prayer is, the God to whom we pray is the source of the power, and He can and will answer us according to His perfect will and timing. When we are intentional and, with focus and passion, pray for someone's needs while asking nothing for us, God does far more than we can even imagine. Prayer is another way we add value to people.

When you are part of an organization's prayer ministry, who are you supposed to call on? Well, everyone who has contacted you in any way. The question I would ask if I was having coffee with you now would be, why would you add them to your mail list and not your prayer list? It is my privilege to call one-hundred percent of them and just say, "This is Tom, and I am calling just to say thanks for the (call, request for help, etc.) and the opportunity to pray for you. It's our way of saying thanks for contacting us." More time than not, if they do not hang up—and some do, because they think it's a scam—they are skeptical, and honestly, some start crying at this point and/or say something like, "You have got to be kidding me." A few say, "You just want to pray for me? I have never received a call like this, even from my church." This is sad, but true. Remember the twenty percent?

So, how often should we call them? A reasonable goal is to call them once a quarter over a year. Most of the time, you'll leave a massage. However, if you truly value them, you want to keep on trying to connect with them directly. Remember, a message left in voicemail can be just as effective as one given in person.

In every organization where there was a prayer ministry, we ended up hiring a full-time associate whose role description is simple and direct: "Your privilege is to pray for people. You are never to ask for a dime—if you do, you're fired." That is it!

Each day, this person calls people and just prays with them and adds value to them. That's it. Sounds easy, right? It's actually quite difficult. For one thing, associates like this are like needles in haystacks; I have no idea why, they just are. Those who are called to this kind of ministry are highly relational, and after making a dozen calls and talking to voicemail on ten of those calls, they are drained and lose energy quickly if they do not talk to a live human.

As the leader of the organization, you'll need to keep reminding them that a voice message is a wonderful opportunity to give an encouraging word, and God's timing factors into when they hear it. You must also help them remember the impact they are making.

Just this past year, we had people actually calling back for prayer when they hit a hard spot. All because of that particular associate's influence and impact. These inbound petition calls resulted in ongoing conversations; the associate prayed for them, connected them to local churches, and helped them see the value of their local church. You name the topic, and it was prayed about and discussed—adding value to the caller.

When done consistently, "with clean hands and a pure heart" as scripture puts it, a prayer ministry will produce additional income. There, I said it. The law of reciprocal proportions kicks in here—but do *not* measure it, nor count on it. If you do, you will end up with a formula, and your motives will slip into a place where they will be calculated. God will withdraw the law. As one organization leader told me, "We tried a prayer ministry, but the costs outweighed the income, so we dropped it."

The moment you move this to the development column, it becomes a transaction—and you are no longer valuing people at the level I am suggesting. It's evident that your value is placed on your income. A prayer ministry cannot be tied in any way to the funds you need to raise—period.

TELL YOUR STORY, NOT YOUR STATISTICS

There's an episode of the U.S. version of television show, "The Office," where the regional sales managers are meeting their new corporate boss in New York. Their supervisor has asked them to prepare presentations to introduce their respective branches of Dunder Mifflin.

The other managers are presenting facts, figures, statistics, charts, profit and loss statements, that sort of thing. When Michael Scott, the lead character, presents his, it is a rough slice-of-life video that introduces his team, what they're about, and a nice, soft U2 song playing in the background while he narrates. It's obvious Michael enjoyed depicting the "slower pace" of his office, and it was obvious by the look on his supervisor's face that he didn't understand what she'd tasked him to do.

Maybe Michael's presentation missed his boss's point, but in relational terms, he was spot-on. He wanted to introduce the office's vibe, intention, team, what they did, what they valued, how close they were. . . and with the show being a television comedy, he did it in a funny way, even if he didn't see it that way.

If you are transitioning to be more relational, you may be part of an organization where the general public will be suspicious of your intentions, at least initially. It's the twenty percent dilemma—most people are not used to non-profits engaging them and adding value to them. They are used to the eighty percent, where they are being asked to add value to the non-profit. If your organization has been known for being highly transactional—inventing crises, sending mass emails every week or even every day, pushing people for more—you need to own this as part of its past. No doubt some may ask, "Haven't you raised enough money yet?"

Remember, you are accountable and as a leader, you are to be transparent. Make a point to ask yourself, "Am I really a person who values people? Am I being genuine? Is this *really* part of who I am?" And answer that honestly.

Next, consider where your board of directors or your executive committee or some level above the chief stewardship officer needs to be engaged in more of the path to the win than constantly checking to see if the numbers are up and whether the budget was met this month. There have to be more conversations with the chief stewardship officer on how the organization arrived at those numbers: How much value did we add the people? Give me a story—don't just tell me what you did. Give me a story that exemplifies what you did. I don't want to know the plan. I want to know the *story* that the plan produced. I think those are the two big things that keep us on track—and God is responsible for everything else, including the attitudes others have about your organization.

Tell the story, and tell it succinctly. Some of you may not be as creative as Michael Scott—you may be more analytical, so here are just some guidelines to help you figure out how to tell the story succinctly. First, when you tell a story, it needs to be less than two minutes; in fact, if you can keep it to a minute or less, that's even better. One of the big hurdles when developing the story is that you cannot give all the details in sixty seconds. And that's a hurdle for a lot of people because they can't be accurate in sixty seconds—and they are a hundred percent correct.

You will not be accurate in sixty seconds, but you can paint a picture in people's minds of what took place. The story should tug on their hearts and minds to such a degree that they're willing to at least take the next step and visit the website, click the link, watch the video, or whatever the call to action might be. Two minutes—for your video, your presentation, your conversation. *Two minutes.*

The story should tell how and why you're doing what you're doing. The audience doesn't need a lot of backdrop; they already know you're working with refugees, orphans, or some other mission. They wouldn't be reading your story if they didn't already have an idea of what you do—they just need to get to the heart of what that person *did*. An example of what I might say while presenting a slide, or a linked photograph on a website:

"Here's an 80-year-old gentleman who came to a church in the Beqaa Valley after the Beirut explosion and without being asked, put twenty-five US dollars in the offering plate, which equals a week of his pay. Heart for Lebanon is all about discipleship-making."

You don't have to preface it with, "I've got to tell this story," thinking you have to get an ask in. One more time: *Everybody knows that a non-profit needs money.* That is no secret. You don't have to talk about it. What you have to do is figure out *why* they should be interested in your non-profit in the first place. What are you doing? Don't put an ask in your story at all. Make *the investors* the hero of the story, not your organization. They already know you need funds to operate.

SO, WHEN *CAN* WE ASK?

Is there ever a time when it's appropriate for a relational person to ask an investor for money? That's a question I get asked frequently. If not now . . . *when?*

I usually respond with, "No, there's never a time to go out and say, 'I need money,' because if you're doing what you're supposed to be doing, and you have the story that proves you're doing what you said you were going to do, people will respond to it."

Is there a time in the conversation, however, where you should mention money? Yes—when it's part of the normal conversation.

For example, I was on the phone a couple of weeks ago with an investor and he said, "I hear the country of Lebanon is in brutal shape with the coronavirus?" I went through all the crises that they were having with the pandemic. And he wanted to know how we were helping, so I replied, "We're providing 1,000,000 face masks and other PPE. It's our response and how we care for people. It's about a $70,000 project." Then I told him how the refugees were helping us make masks, and so forth, and so on.

The point is, yes, the money was *part* of a conversation—but it wasn't the *crux* of the conversation. I didn't throw that in there because I wanted him to write a check, I was answering his questions.

But what if it's not part of an actual conversation? What if you're working on a banner ad, or a video? For instance, if you have a capital campaign, you could end a video or a story by saying, 'we only have thirty percent of our goal to go,' or something like that. There is a place where you can mention things, but it shouldn't be the highlight of the story.

You should not be doing everything that you can do to get the next dollar out of somebody. You want it presented as informational, rather than asking. It's not a game we play—it should come from a pure heart that values people and values the relationship.

SAVE FOR THE RAINY DAYS

I've spent a great deal of time talking about accountability and transparency at the individual and organizational levels; but I haven't spent as much time on financial stewardship, so I need to address what may seem obvious. As you move to be more relational, you should expect a short-term dip in your financials. You are turning a ship, not a speedboat, so there are ways you can navigate this shortfall.

Make sure you have enough in reserves to supplement the loss anywhere from eighteen months to two years. It may not take you that long to turn the ship, but plan on it anyway. None of us, organizationally, lives paycheck-to-paycheck, or ask-letter to ask-letter. Once you have margins, you can begin to make this shift. There's nothing wrong with a savings account.

Here's a principle that non-profits tend to forget, or people who fund non-profits tend to forget, or both: Non-profits aren't non-profits because they don't make a profit; non-profits are non-profit because they get a tax exemption that allows them to be a non-profit. Our profit needs to come in two areas:

- Yes, we need to show a profit on the financial sheet.

- We also need to make a profitable story that proves our investments are producing the outcomes we say we're out to produce.

When you combine the two, you have accountability. You also have transparency, because people can see it, read it, and feel it. They can see the financial sheet. We have to be good stewards of our time and resources to produce the outcomes for the ministry.

From day one, Heart for Lebanon, a ministry I co-founded, saved ten percent of everything that came in. We did so until we hit a financial amount the Board of Directors felt was enough to respond to a major crisis. When something goes terribly wrong in Lebanon, when some major event happens, we have funds to respond to that need immediately. This will buy us time to refill the accounts.

I don't want to be in a position where I must raise the money before I can respond to the need—do you?

Now I've already stated that it's significant that the prayer arm of an organization be kept separate from development, and why prayer associates who ask for money should be fired. You may be thinking, "Wow, Tom, those are both kind of extreme." Hear me out.

The tension comes down to the purity of the heart: *Am I really thanking you for what you did? Or am I thanking you for what you did so I can get more?*

You can't set somebody up to fail. In either case, it would be very tempting for the department or that individual to say, "I won, because I phrased my thank-you so eloquently they are going to send us a check for fifty dollars," or whatever the case. That's not a win, and that's not why you're thanking people. Here's a zinger for some of you: *Receipts, even with a story attached, should not be looked at as a thank-you. Same for bulk letters and emails.* They are not personal.

If someone takes the time to personally send you a financial investment—particularly when they have other options—you owe them a personal thank-you. *This is living in the twenty percent.*

We are thanking people because of a pure *want, a desire,* to thank them. If someone checks their caller ID and sees it's you calling, you don't want them saying, "Oh, they're calling, claiming they just want to thank me. But then they're going to ask me for . . ." That's not building a relationship. Nor is it an authentic expression of gratitude.

So let's position our associates for success. Let's build a wall of protection around them, and let them know the terms of that protection, including the consequences.

That doesn't mean that if someone, over the course of a thank-you call, asks an associate what projects are coming up, that the associate cannot answer them. Of course they can—that's just part of building a relationship. We can answer that question. But the purity of the thank-you, the purity of praying for them isn't there to ultimately slip in an ask for money. We never want to blur those lines.

There are also calls that should be made at least twice a year by your board of directors. Provide your board members a list of investors to call. These calls have a different focus than the prayer calls; the main focus of these calls is to say "thank-you" for your financial investment of any size. Yes, many times it leads to praying with them about some need. Just like the associate calls, the board calls are purely to thank people and ideally, should be done twice a year.

I've had board members in tears after praying with investors. They have shared stories of engagement, how the call made them "richer." By the same token, investors have said things like, "I cannot believe the chairman of your board/secretary/board member called *me*!" These calls make a tremendous impact on investors and board members.

One of the biggest problems we have today in the non-profit world is a very, very wide and general-gap in leadership. Leaders aren't thinking by themselves. They're not looking at, and thinking about, what's best here. They're not asking themselves, *How can I cut through this in a different way?*

Instead, they're looking at it and saying, *How can I cut through this by pouring on more asks?* Or whatever the case may be. Case in point: Giving Tuesday. Really? It's been on-trend the last couple of years, and it's kind of plateaued. It's going to lose steam quickly, because everybody is pushing it to the hilt. I'm not convinced that it really helps your cause. Or social media—along with your birthday, you can attach a cause to it. And make your friends look like cheapskates if they just post a birthday message without giving to your cause. So now we shame friends into giving? That's not very relational.

So, if everybody's asking, we think we've got to do something different in our ask—find a way to up our game. What I'm saying is no, you don't have to up your game. You don't have to get into this competition. Everybody knows you need money. Why are you talking about it?

Let's re-think this—you're accountable, but God is responsible.

EIGHT

OBJECTIONS, CORRECTIONS, AND AUTHENTIC CONNECTIONS

I would like to think that this book has been more of a conversation about valuing people by being relational in *all* areas of your organization—not just how you engage with people who might invest in it.

I want to spend some time revisiting a few things and discussing how to handle objections internally and corrections externally. Why did I wait until the last chapter to bring the latter two to light? Because if you've read this far, you are likely ready to be intentional about being relational, and you're going to need some back-up as you introduce this idea to your closest associates, allow it to permeate your organization's DNA, and demonstrate it to others. Understand that there will be some overlap, some simultaneous action, some linear action, and even some occasional back-tracking.

SKILLS TO MOVE THE CONVERSATION FORWARD

First, a word about valuing the introverted and extroverted associates equally. You may think that extroverts make the best relational engagement strategists, but let me caution you here. You have reasoned that you need a "people person" in the role, and you make a good point; but when we talk about being relational, is that exclusive to extroverts? Stop and re-think this with me.

Extroverts are known for being assertive and enthusiastic, as well as sociable and outgoing. Researchers have even coined the term the "extrovert advantage" to describe the way social environments (pre-Covid-19) help extroverts build relationships that lead to opportunities. While the strategy of a relationship engagement strategist can be great for an extrovert, I would counter with introverts should not be overlooked. Why?

Extroverts network to connect people with their passions in a group setting; they have to talk to people, and they love to talk. Introverts, on the other hand, do not need parties and large groups to network; in fact, the smaller the group, the better. After a half-hour of talking with five to ten people, they are wiped out. They'd rather talk to one or two people to understand their needs and motivations. Their conversations tend to go deeper, quicker. They find ways to connect people to the mission (the "win"). It flows more naturally than with the extrovert.

Introverts do far better with a one-on-one environment than maintaining a large network of relationships and trying to tend to all the needs on each relationship's respective time schedule. That simply doesn't come naturally to them, and it never will; really, they should just stop trying. To be honest, it wears them out emotionally.

Right now, it seems as though I'm still not making the case for the introverts, does it? Extroverts help create those initial connections and:

- Frame the person's wants and needs

- Provide insight into their character and personality

- Identify a potential win-win basis for connection

Introverts, however, do well in moving that relationship forward and building on the connection made.

That said, there are some skills that benefit introverts and extroverts alike as they strive to add value to people.

1. *The Power of Listening*

One of the greatest gifts you can give to anyone is to truly listen. You are making a shift to enrich others—through your own life, and through your organization—and this is where you take the risk of finding out their passions, interests, and goals. Listening, really listening with your heart to a person should be core to your twenty percent—it's a game-changer that very few non-profits are doing.

Encourage those who represent your organization to be themselves, and not try to become someone else. Otherwise, they'll always come across as disingenuous, and people see right through it. There is no win-win in being anyone other you.

That said, introverts and extroverts should push themselves outside of their comfort zones. For example, some extroverts need to learn to speak less and listen more so that they do not come across as know-it-alls. Remember, we want to value people and that, by definition, means we must learn from them by listening to them.

In contrast, some introverts need to push themselves to be a bit more assertive and take the initiative to talk to someone and ask questions. They don't need to pretend to be super-gregarious; they can "brand" this skill with their own personality, as long as the conversation is genuine and they are using the incredible gift most of them possess—*listening*.

In most cases, listening comes much easier for an introvert. People are naturally attracted to people who actively listen to them; it shows you care. Regardless of whether you align more with introverts or extroverts, any time you have a conversation, do not be in a hurry. If you're meeting in person, leave your mobile phone in the car (along with your watch). If you're speaking by phone, do not get distracted with other things, like checking email or having another conversation with someone who walks into the room—the person on the line can sense you're not paying attention. Slow down, take the time, and truly listen. When you do, you communicate that you value that person. It can be life-changing for them and you.

2. Take The Conversation to Social Media

As I'm writing this, we are (hopefully) emerging from the Covid-19 pandemic. It's been a difficult eighteen months, and many of us remain hesitant and vulnerable about "waking up" the world. For those of us who did not suffer from the virus directly, it presented a challenging opportunity to get creative with our communication.

Being introverted or shy doesn't have to hold you back. In fact, technology and social media have automatically allowed us to build, maintain, and expand relationships with very little hassle. Connecting with others on social media, Zoom, FaceTime, and other platforms is arguably easier than in person. Live events can be hosted online and provide global access to individuals who are equally eager to connect and discover. The cost is minimal, except for the cost of the time you spend listening. Make initial contact online, and once you're comfortable, reach out over the phone, or schedule a one-on-one meeting. Challenge yourself to be better than your weaknesses. Make a habit of conquering your fears, and soon you'll question what it was you were afraid of in the first place. Remind yourself that your non-profit deserves to be seen and heard by others.

3. *Yes, You Can Grow Relationships Online*

Since March of 2020, I have rarely attended any networking or group events/meetings of any size in person. I have done most of my significant relationship engagement online. I'll reach out with a short, but well-targeted invite to a Zoom call to discuss our passion—no one has turned me down yet. And when I do attend in-person events or meetings, it's never been more than four or five of us total, so I'm not sure if that qualifies as an event.

In either case, I'll often keep the conversation short and ask more questions than I did in the pre-covid-19 environment. I leave ample time for a question-and-answer session. After each encounter, I follow up with each individual who attended the call and continue the conversation via email.

Recently, I hosted a Zoom meeting with a group that resided in a time zone with a 3-hour time difference. So they arrived at their 7:00 p.m. local time, but it was 10:00 p.m. in my neck of the woods. After the 35-minute "prepared presentation," we opened the Q & A portion . . . and it lasted two hours. It was fantastic!

4. *Get Used to Getting Out of Your Comfort Zone*
Approaching new people and public speaking scared me more than probably anything else for the first part of my life. Fast forward to today—I have no problem with meeting new people, and really enjoy speaking in front of others.

We all have our own comfort zones, and it hurts to get out of them. For many, meeting new people is *way* out of their comfort zone. The leap is just too big to take. Instead of taking a leap, I encourage people to try taking steps. Even baby steps—small things that may seem a little uneasy at first. In most cases, you'll realize it's not as bad as you thought—you likely built it up in your head to be far more intrusive/uncomfortable/scarier than it actually is. Give yourself some grace if you stumble . . . and accept that you may stumble, just like toddlers do when they take their first steps.

Allow me to share with you something I started doing a few years back that has helped me retain focus and allowed me to listen to others. When I noticed that in just about every Q&A, someone asked, "What does your organization do?" I decided to re-think my response. I created a log of "boilerplate" stories that personalize and humanize our mission. Stories are interesting; stories invite questions, and continue the conversation. Let me be clear; I do not memorize a script. That's playing a game, being transactional. I have a few stories that are especially meaningful and diverse so that I am prepared to share the one that fits best with my investor or group. Having something like that ready, I am not spending my time cycling through a "rolodex" of possibilities instead of paying attention to the person I'm chatting with. I keep the story simple, like we discussed in Chapter 7. Most non-profits, when asked, will spout off mission statements, key initiatives, statistics, but stories are the non-profit currency of today. They tend to add value to others, in every conversation—every tweet, every email, etc. If you keep a couple of stories in your back pocket, ready to share, that's living in the twenty percent.

When you look at everything you do through the lens of "adding value to others," you will be relational in the entire organization.

THE TRIANGLE APPROACH

If you look at the triangle, which side could you drop and it remain a triangle?

The "triangle approach" is a visual that illustrates the relational philosophy. When applied, it accounts for adding value to people from three places: the mission win, associate members, and investors. All three support each other, all three are required to show up in a relational organization that would still prove that your DNA, the core of who you are, the ethos of who you are, is a relational person and you care about someone else.

As soon as you drop one of those three, the one dropped indicates that you don't really care about people. All three have to work together. All three have to be together to work.

As we implement a relational philosophy, we need to ask ourselves before we start a new relationship:

- Do I value this person unconditionally?

- Do I value this person period, and it does not matter if I get a check or not?

- Do I just desire to enrich this person anyway I can?

- Do I want to change this person, or do I want to learn from this person?

A relationship then begins when you engage with them, so it's best to address these questions in your mind and heart as early as possible during this period. As you get to know the person better, you'll understand what their passion and dreams are, maybe even their calling and end goals.

Our world has changed dramatically since March 2020. For non-profits, *now* is the time to review and to re-think their strategies. To keep on doing what we've always done will not allow us to do what we've accomplished in the past. We can't go back, because the world has changed.

This is particularly urgent for those operating in a faith-based space. We must get back to aligning our values with what God values—and God values people. Faith-based or not, we should value people. In doing so, we need to trend away from words like *fundraising* and *donor* and shift our focus to relationships.

Make no mistake: All of this must start with you, the leader. If you're not convicted in your heart that this is who you are, who you want to be, and who you want to be remembered as being, you will not be in a position to influence others to do the same.

I deeply believe that people have value. Therefore, words like *donor* denotes someone who gives blood, gives one time, or is involved in limited transactional fundraising. I don't care for that word because as soon as I hear it, I think of a non-profit carwash, golf game, skeet shoot, bake sale, or some other transactional event.

When you meet a person, have a conversation with them, see if you have some kind of connection. If you do, suggest another conversation. Understandably, you'll have a better connection with some than others. When that happens, and following many more conversations, you'll likely begin a relational partnership of some sort. Regardless of whether that happens or not, relational people value *all* people who come across our paths until we mutually agree that we can't add value to them, or they don't want value added to them.

The challenge for many is the acceptance when there is no passion-match. That is the other edge to the relational sword—when it's rewarding, it's very rewarding, but when it's not, it's hard to let go. You see, transactional fundraising is not very personal, while relationships are very personal. So usually, when you arrive at a crossroads in the conversation where there's not really a passion-match, the leader has to end the relationship. That is healthy and prevents you from experiencing a desperation to hang on and tip-toe into transactional game-playing.

When you attempt to put the word *relational* in front of fundraising, you're going to put strain on your relationships. You'll be on some sort of psychological treadmill every day, desperate to come up with some project or crisis to elicit emergency funding. You become desperate to continue a relationship that's not really there because your mind and heart are not aligned to add value to them—instead, you need something from them (usually, their money, but it could be their power, their influence, etc.).

Truly relational people do not want anything from anyone. We want something *for* them. I'm not saying you won't make mistakes, or need to fine-tune your heart and mind—but I am saying that if you jump on that treadmill, you'll stay on it because of the low fulfillment rates. You will constantly be searching for more money, dreaming up a different crisis or another project . . . it's an endless cycle, and many organizations live there and have that mindset.

I sat in a meeting recently with one such organization, and they were very pleased to report that they reached 83 percent of the previous month's budget. They think that's a win when in fact, they are measuring the wrong thing.

Why is 83 percent not a win? Because you're looking at it from a dollars and cents point of view. You're not looking at the person or persons responsible and you're not considering the privilege you have as a chief stewardship officer to help inspire people, to give them a greater story, to add value to them—something *more fulfilling to them* than they could ever imagine.

Every single human desires to be part of something that's bigger, something that makes a greater impact than they can dream of making by themselves. Non-profit organizations have an incredible opportunity to walk with people and lead them into a relationship around a mission and a vision that can be accomplished better together than we could alone. When we can do that, we've helped that person have a better story to tell, a better future. A growing relationship that's built on trust will, at some point, lead them to ask, "Can *I* help *you* in any way?"

If the answer is *yes*, we respond that way truthfully. Not because we want the money, but because we want that person's future to be better. Maybe they never thought about helping Muslims. Maybe they never thought about helping the homeless shelter down the street. Maybe they thought your organization was totally funded by government grants or by a parent organization or you had plenty of volunteers to assist you in new initiatives. If they start to get a visual of how their story could connect with yours, you have a wonderful opportunity to connect. *They* become the hero of the story—not the founder, president, or CEO of the non-profit. You're adding value to the person by expanding their footprint and their future.

I want to detour for a couple of paragraphs here, but I promise it's purposeful to the greater topic. If you're in one of those positions—founder, CEO, president—you are used to recognition. You are used to shaking hands, receiving acknowledgements, getting all the credit. So being relational may take some serious ego-shedding, and you need to be honest with yourself about that. In fact, I would say the main reason most non-profits are transactional and not relational is because someone's ego is standing in the way. You're not adding value to a person if all you're doing is flattering them enough to take something from them or manipulate them into giving you something. Or even if you're not actively flattering or manipulating them—you're just doing all the taking. It's not relational. It's not even close to being relational.

Ask yourself some honest questions: *Am I really valuing people? Am I really evaluating that person when I'm willing to settle for a financial gift, but I'm not willing to help them accomplish what they believe their future should look like?* Even if the honest answer is, "I have been. But I don't want to do that anymore," you have a starting point for changing your DNA. There is such a thing as having confident humility—no one is asking you to assume a weak persona.

Now back to our regularly scheduled topic: Even though ending a relationship may not be what you want to do, it's the right thing to do if you're starting to manipulate something to please the investor. That will always get you in trouble—not to mention that's operating without integrity. So, you have to have a hard conversation. Over my lifetime of experience, I've had a couple of those. Out of respect, I make an appointment with that person and sit down with them. I usually say something like, "I've got to apologize for something. I feel like I'm manipulating a story to please you, and we can't go down this road. I've just got to end this."

At this point, I would have ended the transaction of getting the investor's support, but my goal is to *keep the relationship*. So, I never want to give up on the relationship. In fact, I might not talk to this person for six months because of where life takes me, but I still communicate with those whom I've had this challenging conversation with. We're still friends on Facebook; we're not enemies. If you're honest with the investor, believe it or not, they don't get angry. They might stop supporting you or investing in your organization, but their opinion of you will be that you're a person of integrity and your trustworthiness just went up about four hundred percent—because most people aren't willing to have that conversation. *That's* living in the twenty percent.

OBJECTIONS AND
HOW TO HANDLE THEM

We've spent a great deal of time talking about creating a relational culture—but we haven't addressed how to fully implement it at the organizational level. Why would I choose to put this at the end the book when seems to belong at the beginning?

Most of what I've relayed so far has been directed at *you*—your own behaviors, your actions, your thoughts, your heart. That twenty-percent part is essential, and must transition within yourself before any implementation can take place in your organization. You must decide in your own heart and mind where you are with this before you can influence others to be relational.

So when it comes to implementing a relational philosophy, a leader can't just walk in and tell his team, "We're going relational." And if you are still thinking this is some sort of calculated strategy that can be implemented and measured with timelines, graphs, and flow charts, that's not being relational. So, what might be a good roadmap— one with detours, bridges, and optional routes—for accomplishing this?

You'll need the trust and support from your board and key leadership teams. Be transparent about your role in what brought your organization to this point: "Listen, I'm making a major switch because I believe I was wrong. I have been very transactional in my own thinking. We've got to make an adjustment here to be more relational. I've already started with myself and want my associates to embrace this, because this is a deep conviction I have—this is something that's part of me now." Get the board on board.

Eventually, your associates will notice a change, even if they can't put their finger on it. Something's just "different." And they are influenced by this . . . so your investors take notice. What has changed (besides not bombarding them with requests for money)? There's been a subtle shift, but it seems to be making a major turn. As people come into your path, you're taking more time with them and not asking anything of them. Remember, it's a triangle of success.

And this is where the water gets murky, because at some point, someone is going to raise their hand and say, "Yeah, I like the idea of being relational, but the budget has to be met. And I don't see any big push for that? You're not talking to people about money anymore, you're talking to them about going to have *coffee*."

This is likely the biggest objection, and it is murky. No, you cannot craft a strategy or timeline for becoming relational . . . but in my experience, I can tell you that on average, it takes a full two years before you start to see any return. In terms of preparation, I will advise you to have the funds or budgets in place to weather two years of this shift. You may have personnel changes, etc., that must be factored into the budgeting—though I pray that won't be the case. There may be other ways to quantify your steps, but being relational and focusing on the twenty percent does not lend itself to a bunch of statistics. This may be a challenge for some of the more analytical personalities on your team.

The second objection may be more subtle, because it has more to do with you specifically and less about your organization. You may be the type of leader who does not have the best reputation; you are not viewed as someone who is compassionate and caring. The objection comes from the distrust your associates and investors have; they're not necessarily going to say, "Why are you being so nice all of a sudden?" They're just going to avoid you even more, convinced that you're just going through a temporary phase of kindness.

This is where some of that confident humility needs to be sustained. If your past behavior has given them reason to distrust you, you have a much bigger problem that needs to be addressed. It will take some time to build back the trust that should have been there all along. Do not skip this step, or think it's less of a priority. If you don't have the trust of board or your team, you will get nowhere.

Why can't you just soldier on and hope they'll get there? Simple. There will be times when the chair, the finance officer, or someone else comes to you and says, "This is murky, and I'm not sure this is going to work. I mean, the trends aren't looking good." And they'll be right in their assessment of the numbers and maybe even the lack of clarity . . . and your only response will be, "You've got to trust me on this. I believe in this, we are going to change, and we're going to be relational. We're going to stick with this."

But visualize this in big, huge, flashing bright-red neon lights: *This isn't a game.*

You can't play the game called "I'm Building Relationships to Get Money." It cannot be that, ever. It has to be a part of your DNA. Of course you can believe what money can do, and believe in the principle that people will respond because they care. . . . but not because you asked. And that's where problems arise, because we start playing a game with the intent of getting money. If you think like that, you might as well go back to your flow charts, graphs, and crisis-of-the-month clubs. Build relationships because it's the right thing to do, period.

Wise leaders use discernment, so I think it's perfectly normal to expect some hesitation about what "being relational" is, even if it's the tired, "Well, that's not how we're used to doing things," sort of objections. In fact, you may have associates who say, "Yeah, this isn't my cup of tea, I'm not doing this. It's not going to work."

When you've changed your own DNA and are now trying to do the same within your organization, there are two big agenda objections that you'll run into. And they're huge. And they're why most people give up on it really fast.

The first one is that it will take too long. "We need money. Now. Yesterday, in fact." They object because the rate of return will be slower (I don't like referring to it as "rate of return," but in comparison to transactional fundraising, I'll use it here). You'll hear this objection as "this is too hard," when in fact, it's a fear of the unknown.

You might also hear this objection as, "We don't like to/ want to change people." People actually love to change. We may not realize this, but we do. We go out and buy a new shirt, new dress, or new shoes. Why? Because we want to change what we have. We buy new cars, new homes, go on vacation for a change of scenery. We change for the possibility of having something better, something different, something unique. The challenge is in the transition, from old to new—when we're in that neutral zone, the unknown zone. That's where we get hung up: *How* do I move from this?

The 'this' is familiar, expected, and sometimes, comfortable, and easy. Your board and your associates may 'get it,' they just don't want to walk through the neutral zone to get it. As leaders, we have to steward that neutral zone really, really, really, really—did I say really?—well.

Likely, your board will take some convincing, no matter how much they trust you. Make a point to share and show the change that will be developing in the future, the direction you are headed. Kindly reassure them that there are no plans to drop all the fundraising efforts at once. You don't want to scare anyone in the neutral zone. This is a slow transition, a step-by-step process that moves intentionally and stewards a healthy neutral zone. Sometimes, it helps to have an outside consultant walk the organization through it; they can assist with any blind spots, and help identify potential stumbling blocks.

So the first big objection is "We don't have enough money." The second one is, "I don't know if people will buy into it."

One thing's for certain: If you announce it, they will not buy into it. But if you show them first and grow into it, then the ones who are truly relational will embrace it. (Stay with me, later in the chapter I will show you how to add value to those who do not embrace it.)

Before you take any of those initial steps to transition your organization—steps that will put them in the neutral zone—don't call a meeting and announce that you're making the switch. Instead, show them by your actions:

"Hey, that was a great job."

"You handled that really well."

"You went over and above here."

"What is the best way for me to support you here?"

"Are there things I could do differently that would help you?"

I would also get into the habit of referring to them as *associates* as often as possible, and slowly move away from using the word *staff*, and maybe even *team*. There will come a time when that's important, but for now, just start changing your vocabulary.

You see, everyone gets treated equally. If you don't treat everyone equally, what do you do with Jesus? If you don't treat everyone equally, what do you do with the second chapter of James 2:1? Paul tells us that Jesus, the Son of God, died for everyone—not just for the wealthy, or just for the poor, or just for those who go to church—no, Paul says Jesus died for everyone.

James says we are not to pre-judge anyone. This is where intentionality is a big deal because it requires that we steward it. I'm not saying that relationships are easy; when my wife and I were newlyweds, we hit a few bumps in the road, just like every other pair of newlyweds. Forty-eight years later, I can tell you it was well worth it.

Another word of caution I've touched on previously with regard to investors, but also want to underscore here within your organization: *There is a fine line in being relational that should never be crossed.* You must be careful not to take your relationships too far. This happens when you get way too personal, and the messiness of it is that each person is different so therefore, each fine line will be different. As chief stewardship officers, we need to be conscious of where that line might be with each one. And if it's going too far, we need to be the ones who—without making a big deal of it—pull it back.

"Okay, Tom," you may be saying, "but we still need money *now*. Being relational sounds like something we need to explore, but we're in the red this quarter. Is there a way to gradually become relational?" And my answer is yes . . . and no.

You're either relational or you're not. There is no "kinda-sorta" or "parts and pieces" to this. If you're a relational person, you add value to people. It's what you feel at your very core.

Becoming a relational organization, however, is a gradual process. You do, in fact, ride two horses at the same time for a couple of years, especially if you're changing from highly transactional actions to being highly relational. There is a transition. You can't just say, "Tomorrow morning at eight o'clock, we shut off our transactional approach and start being relational." That will not work. For one thing, it's disingenuous; it points back to the question I asked earlier in the book about the sign you see on someone's forehead. When you're relational, you want to value them by virtue of them being a human being and add more value to them by helping them discover and connect with whatever their passion is. And that takes time—time to explain to your board, your associates, and others you meet why you may have been more transactional before, and you're relational now. You can't explain that in a mass email.

The transition will not be easy. Being relational is fulfilling, yes, but difficult work—and the overwhelming majority of it, for the first six to eight months, will come straight from you, the chief stewardship officer. You will set the pace of how well it works. From there, it seeps into all the other areas—the phone calls, the personal visits, etc.

Now even though I may not be familiar with your organization, my guess is that a lot of your development associates are far more relational than they're being credited for; consider calling them "engagement" instead of "development." Anyway, this transition will not be that big of a deal for some of them.

It will be a bigger deal, however for the marketing department, since they want to churn out a big-ask letter every other month or every two weeks. Their work will change dramatically; for starters, the tone of their communication will change. All the letters, emails, social media will focus on adding value to people. Not a letter that tells some story that's going to move them emotionally to give from their pocketbook. That will come later. The first order of business is always to add value to the recipient.

While your marketing department may question the dramatic turn of events, sometimes you may have an associate who is not on board, for whatever reason. When that happens, it's likely because of two or three things that have not taken place.

One is likely because they have not bought into the *why*. They understand the how—the *how* is not the problem, and in fact, they may understand the *how* better than others and can see how challenging the transition will be. It's the *why*—why are we doing this?—that's the problem.

If your temper is flaring over someone's lack of enthusiasm or willingness, and you're ready to have a strong word with them about it, then I can already tell you that you are not modeling it the right way—because a relational person would not respond that way. Remember our discussion about "confidence with humility"? Before you assume they are being stubborn, consider that they don't understand it because you don't model it. They need to be convinced that this is the way to go, and that will take some extra time and effort.

I've known people who really didn't want to be relational in their professional relationships. "If God's in charge," they explained, using my own words and scripture to counter their own *why*. "God will take care of it. I don't have to do anything. If God's in charge, then whatever will happen will happen, because God's in charge." You may face a similar response from some of your associates, and that's the end of it right there. That's not being a good steward, and that's not adding value by building relationships—that's you being taken advantage of. And God told us not to do that. We're not to take advantage of people because we should value people too much for that—and in this case, whether we report to them or they report to us, the value placement should be reciprocal.

Eventually, they have to understand the value of relationships, whether they are introverted or extroverted. You may be faced with a frank discussion about how the organization values people, and explain how their role and responsibilities contributes to that. If they don't buy into it, then you're going to have to have the hard conversation that this isn't working. That doesn't mean you cast them out or shame them. That's not adding value to them. Ask them, "Can you help me understand why you don't see that your work at this non-profit is adding value to people? Because if it's not, then we need to find a place where you can add value to people outside of this organization." Sincerely try to help them if it's apparent that the latter is the correct call to make. They may get angry and refuse your help, but you try anyway. Lead with confidence, but do so with humility.

Those are hard conversations because every non-profit wants to be known for adding value to people. That's why they're a non-profit. It's very difficult to have people on your team who don't value people; but if their values don't align with the organization's, you are doing them a disservice to try and force that when it's not going to work. Add value to them by helping them connect with their passion, same as anyone else.

CORRECTIONS AND SEPARATIONS

One of the organizations that I work with had a significant investor who, with one phone call, stopped supporting that organization. The reason that he was not fulfilling the rest of his investment was that he perceived that the organization was no longer doing what he was passionate about.

While I could have argued the point and provided data and other resources to substantiate that we most certainly did support what he was passionate about, I chose not to get into the discussion about the passion-match. I wanted to do my best to keep the relationship. The funds were secondary.

What's interesting about that story is four weeks later, that organization received a personal check from him. Enclosed with the check was a little note that said, *I appreciate the way Tom handled the situation and I'd like to meet with him the next time he is in town.* Which I did. We had a great conversation but never talked about money or the situation. It's a rebuilding of a relationship, not about who's right or wrong,

I believe all organizations, whether they know it or not, yearn for a relationship with their investors, because deep down, they really value people. They are just desperate for funding or they never really stopped to take the time to think about what they really value. Relationships require a lot of time and work from you as a steward. We must value the person, over their wealth and what you think they can do for you. It's not about you! It's about meeting their needs—not yours.

I talk to everyone who comes across my path. It's my God-given responsibility to do that, but I already know that I won't connect with everyone. God's not asked me to discern that in advance of meeting them, so I talk to everyone, and I try my best to treat all people with respect and dignity. So, how much do you invest in a relationship?

Well, I think the answer to that is, how much value do you want to add to their life? The more you've invested, the greater the return, and over time, a relationship compounds and contracts. So, what happens if the person doesn't want to meet any longer? If they're worn out and tired? Or if they've decided their passion no longer aligns with your mission?

In the example I described above, we maintained their respect and our dignity—no one left that conversation angry or hurt. People are counting on you to speak the truth and to keep your promises. This reflects your character and ultimately who you are. They do not expect perfection, but they do expect honesty, kindness, and follow-through. This is how you build trust, and trust is the lifeblood of all relationships. I'm not here to tell you that these kinds of conversations are easy. They are extremely difficult, regardless of the amount of time involved. But you know, you'll never forget the story—and neither will they. Steward your words carefully, as this may be the lasting imprint you make on their lives.

If you're relational, your focus is not on fundraising—it's on the relationship. If your 'donor strategy' is relational fundraising, you're not relational. You either want to add value to people or you want to schmooze with those who will give you money. You can't really do both; it's one or the other. Most organizations that claim they do relational fundraising are really just out for a check, and they're using the strategy of a relationship rather than wanting the best future for that person. The goal should be to add value to that person, and work with them to build a relationship that's on their timetable. You can't rush the process.

Remember my question early in the book? *What about the process?* Here are some questions to consider:

- Everyone is worth talking to; are you willing to talk to everyone who comes across your path?

- Are you willing to spend time with people?

- Is there a connection?

- Are you willing to put the energy and resources into building that connection into a relationship?

- Are you willing to care about what they care about?

- Do you want to know what they dream about?

- Do you want to know what hurts them, or how they hurt?

- Do you want to just pick up the phone as a friend and call them to ask how they are doing?

- Are you willing to pray with them and pray for them?

No relationship ever moves at the exact same pace. Some take weeks, others take months, others may take years—it all depends on the other person's schedule, not on yours. This is where trust is developed, and when you get to the trust phase, which is really about showing your organization's integrity and your character, then they know you're not playing games or flattering them to manipulate money out of them.

Trust leads to partnership and collaboration. It's at that point where they may say something like, "I know what your organization does, and I think I want to help you somehow. How might I do that? What kind of projects do you have going on right now?" If you've been adding value to them, then you already know what they dream about, what they care about, and what they really are passionate about. You probably have a project or budget item that connects to their passion. See if they want to do it or not. No pressure, no push, no big numbers, no nothing.

And if nothing comes to mind immediately, let them know you'll be looking around to see where they can help. This reinforces what they already know—that you are trustworthy and not in it for the money. We have to be okay with this going either way. You can't think short-term, and you can't force something out of a person that will benefit the organization more than them. Why is it always better to have an emphasis on valuing people?

Whether or not they have a foundation of faith, if someone feels valued, they want to give back. They want to help. They want to be part of something greater than themselves. And eventually, they will step up. And sadly, that's true even when they do this as a result of flattery and manipulation—because we often don't recognize the difference until we have been used. So as relational leaders who value people and operate with integrity, we must be very careful to focus on adding value and not resorting to what amounts to trickery to skew the outcome.

Now here's the benefit that will drive you (and, word of caution, be very careful not to turn this into a formula): In time, if you build a relational organization that does relational work, top to bottom, by adding value to people, the financial resources will be provided. When the passions match, the resources arrive. And believe me, it *is* a step of faith.

It's not totally Müller and Taylor, but it's not Moody, either. It's somewhere in-between.

We're telling a story about the investors becoming the hero in the story—not the organization. They will continue to add value because it's intrinsic to human nature that if we bless someone, they will want to bless back. And you haven't asked for a dime.

Is there any occasion where the dollars and cents have to matter more?

Absolutely, one-hundred percent, *no*.

There is never a reason to raise the money over and above caring for people. If you find yourself going there, it's time to rethink what you value and get back to the twenty percent that makes you and your organization different.

You need to be sold on the fact that your mission—and the organization's mission—is really all about building godly relationships. Are you willing to pay the price to value all people and what they might need? You may need to go to your board, executive committee, inner circle to help you really answer that question, because that is a significant, unique calling. Don't brush off the process.

When you build authentic relationships, you will build significant trust and that trust will put change in your pocket . . . but it will take time to build. Make it personal first—it starts with you. If you're not relational in your own life, your organization will struggle with it, too.

I have way too many cautionary tales of organizations who really desired to be relational in their fundraising, and it never worked. I wonder if this is one reason that in a recent issue of *Forbes* magazine, there was a headline that read: "45% of Non-profit Employees to Seek New Jobs By 2025." This is one of the biggest challenge's facing non-profits face today; true engagement strategists are difficult to find, and turnover has become a major problem for many non-profits. One contributing factor is that we are trying to limit the relational philosophy to one area of our organization and it rubs hard against the rest of the organization that is not. My suggestion is to stop the tension and let the entire organization be relational.

It's true in any relationship—when we believe the best in a person, it usually brings out the best in them. That's not to say that we don't have blind spots; we all are imperfect, but when someone gently calls out a blind spot, it's because they desire the best for us. We then feel empowered to do almost anything at any time. When we find something to compliment or praise in another person—sincerely, not as flattery—we add value to them, because our honesty enriches them.

A FINAL NOTE FROM TOM

Without question, all non-profits believe they add value to people. The question is, does your non-profit organization add value to people—really? Are your "relationships" really a strategy to get something? Or are you building relationships because it's your DNA, your calling, your mandate to add value no matter what happens.

I believe that as we exit COVID-19, the new pandemic that is emerging is the pandemic of loss. While this pandemic of loss is new, the biggest area of loss started a few years before the coronavirus. Today, it's approaching an epic level. The loss of relationships is having a tremendous negative effect on individuals in every age group and affects every area of a person's life. Relationships are the glue that keep us together, help us process our thoughts, and guide us through life's journey.

All humans in all cultures have an inherent DNA to be "in relationships" in order to be close to other people. To connect and build relationships—this is who we are as humans. Healthy relationships (romantic, friendships, family, organizational, etc.—they all count!) can help make for a healthier and more fruitful life. But what exactly does a healthy relationship look like; whether it's personal or an organizational?

A healthy or positive relationship can be shared between any two people who share the same passion and desire to help each other. Relationships help us with our personal, professional, emotional, and spiritual journeys. In no particular order, people in healthy relationships do these six things daily:

- Listen to each other

- Communicate openly and without judgment

- Trust and respect each other

- Consistently make time for each other

- Remember details about each other's lives

- Engage in healthy activities together

Just to be clear, I am not talking about romantic relationships. I don't believe you have to be romantically involved to enjoy the benefits of a healthy relationship.

As you read this book, you learned a lot about the Law of Reciprocity, which states that when someone does something nice for you (adds value), you will have a deep-rooted, psychological urge to do something nice (add value) to them in return. In many cases, one might reciprocate with a greater gesture, which is far more generous than the original good deed. It's a natural response to a relationship that is growing. However, you must not make a formula out of this law; once you do, you no longer have a relationship.

In reading this book, you may have also come to believe that relationships are a faith-building experience; you arrived at a place where you said, "since I am the chief steward officer of this non-profit organization, I need to work with my confidence in God first." When you do, it takes the pressure off of what you 'must' do. As the chief steward, you then can be more relaxed, more energetic, more creative, and you can stay focused. In fact, your sole focus will be to add value to people.

While this book has hopefully prompted you to rethink, it's the result of that thinking that can and will help you grow your non-profit to a higher level of engagement with people. It will help you to not just add value to people, but add *tremendous* value to people. While the principles in this book are for all non-profits, it's the faith-based organizations that I believe it can help the most.

From my experience and viewpoint, faith-based non-profits have placed a growing confidence on their systems, structures, and formulas similar to our non-faith-based counterparts. This drift has allowed faith-based non-profits to treat and organize their staff, building a machine to bring in what they think they need. They act more like the secular organizations do. Faith-based organizations have, or are losing, the faith aspect; in many cases, they have drifted away from really adding value to people. I have tried to show you examples of why this is true.

What I am really suggesting in this book is that you re-view, re-focus, and reset your organization before you end up with an organizational machine that has to perform to keep your organization going. When you operate at the machine level, you're one small step away from a "monument" mentality which says, *It's all about me.*

I can imagine what your question is now: "So like Hudson Taylor or George Müller, do I just pray and wait? What do I do to meet our needs?"

I would encourage you to read or reread Chapter 7 and 8. However, let me say your spiritual-leadership gut comes into play here big-time; it's why the relational organization starts and stops with you. What's inside your heart and mind is vitally important.

One of my favorite verses from the Bible is this one: "Therefore I say unto you, Take no thought for your life, what ye shall eat, or what ye shall drink; nor yet for your body, what ye shall put on. Is not the life more than meat, and the body than raiment?" –Matthew 6:25 (KJV)

Jesus tells us not to worry about these kinds of things. To which our response is often, "Yeah, but he does not mention *funding* and by the way, what am I supposed to do if we do not have enough money for_____? What if people do not respond?"

It's here where we tend to veer off-track, because we lack the faith-steps of our stewardship responsibility. Our minds—or more accurately, the salesperson who resides in our minds—starts selling us on, "but what if" and, "in case of." We wander over to what the "normal" system does (the eighty percent I've talked about) and our narrative and practice, over time, change. The salesperson in us has taken over, and set us on a course that leads us to think that we are responsible. God says that's the way non-faith people and non-faith organizations think.

Come on—your faith, your confidence is where? Why are you listening to that salesperson, anyway?

Hudson Taylor wrote an editorial that stated: "All God's giants have been weak men, who did great things for God because they reckoned on His being with them." As he looked at himself, Taylor saw nothing but weakness; but as generations of Christians study Taylor's life, they become acquainted with a man who dared to believe the Word of God and by faith, carried the gospel to inland China— where God worked wonders!

"Want of trust is at the root of almost all our sins and all our weaknesses," he wrote in that same editorial, "and how shall we escape it but by looking to Him and observing His faithfulness. The man who holds God's faithfulness will not be foolhardy or reckless, but he will be ready for every emergency."

Faith-based organizations have drifted too far into the world's thinking lane. While it is true Jesus said "believe in me," he also says as soon as you believe, "follow me." His instruction to those who "believe" has never changed; "follow me" in all areas of life.

You might think that being a good steward can be tricky. *How much should we save for a rainy day? How much do we keep in checking? How much do we . . .* well, you get the idea. All good questions. What I am suggesting, however, is that when these thoughts pop-up in our thinking, we take a different, or a "follow me" approach.

It's hard to trust God when the things you think you have control over and that you believe you are responsible for have to be relinquished into His hands.

When you consistently add value to people, your impact will be transformative. For the faith-based chief steward, these words from the Apostle Paul are good to study, ponder, and write their principles on your wall:

> *Let love be without dissimulation. Abhor that which is evil; cleave to that which is good. Be kindly affectioned one to another with brotherly love; in honour preferring one another; not slothful in business; fervent in spirit; serving the Lord; rejoicing in hope; patient in tribulation; continuing instant in prayer; distributing to the necessity of saints; given to hospitality. Bless them which persecute you: bless, and curse not. Rejoice with them that do rejoice, and weep with them that weep. Be of the same mind one toward another. Mind not high things, but condescend to men of low estate. Be not wise in your own conceits. Recompense to no man evil for evil. Provide things honest in the sight of all men. If it be possible, as much as lieth in you, live peaceably with all men. Dearly beloved, avenge not yourselves, but rather give place unto wrath: for it is*

written, Vengeance is mine; I will repay, saith the Lord. Therefore if thine enemy hunger, feed him; if he thirst, give him drink: for in so doing thou shalt heap coals of fire on his head. Be not overcome of evil, but overcome evil with good. –Romans 12:9-21 (KJV)

I'll leave you with this: The number one contender for your faith is money. The most fulfillment you will receive is from building relationships that add value to people, as suggested by the Apostle Paul. No matter what, let go of the systems and structures you have in place to "raise money" and trust God's plan instead. It's much different than what you see around you.

God adds value to you every day—pass it on! My prayer is that this book has added value to you; may it be pivotal in your personal journey and that of your non-profit organization. I would love for our paths to cross so we could continue the conversation. You can contact me via email at *Tom@Relationshipsbreaktherules.com*.

Together we are better!
Tom

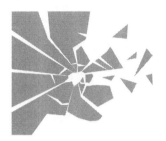

ABOUT
THE AUTHOR

Tom Atema, founder and president of Vertical Horizons Group, has spent 35 years helping some of today's most successful ministries and non-profits achieve greater levels of influence and success. He believes every organization has room to grow, no matter how old it is, how big it is, or how successful it has become.

Having learned a lot about good business practices, the importance of hard work, and the value of partnerships during childhood, Tom spent his early adult years working with his father, in one of the largest and most successful regional dairy distributors in the country. He carried that same work ethic into the non-profit world, where he guided leaders to take themselves and their organizations to the next level in influence, financial support, and people power. Some of the non-profits Tom served during that time include Word of Life Fellowship, Billy Graham Evangelistic Association, EQUIP Leadership Inc., Heart for Lebanon, and 4B Serve.

In his current role as founder and president of Vertical Horizons Group, Tom helps the next generation of leaders keep things moving and achieve their own ministry breakthroughs. A true visionary who prefers the road *not* taken, Tom helps leaders maximize their potential by motivating them to proactively nurture relationships instead of reacting to circumstances. He's a strategic thinker with a proven ability to coach others to become even better than they think themselves capable. As he walks alongside them, Tom helps them see themselves and their organizations more clearly, and coaches them to think strategically, act decisively.

Tom resides in North Carolina with his wife Chris and loves to snowmobile, take walks, spend time with the grandchildren and add value to others.